JOURNAL OF A COMBAT TANKER
Vietnam, 1969

Toby L. Brant

VANTAGE PRESS
New York / Atlanta
Los Angeles / Chicago

FIRST EDTION

Published by Vantage Press, Inc.
516 West 34th Street, New York, New York 10001

Manufactured in the United States of America
ISBN: 0-533-06985-8

Library of Congress Catalog Card No.: 86-90034

This book is dedicated to all of the men and women who gave their lives in the service of their country in Vietnam and to the men and women who were scarred mentally and maimed physically by the horrors of the Vietnam War. This book is also dedicated to the people whose lives are shackled to the bitter memories of Vietnam for all time.

FOREWORD

OFTEN ONE WILL PAUSE in the heat of an adventure story, gaze into that formless sounding board for our thoughts, and wonder, "Could this really have happened? Is there really enough stretch in reality for such as this?" If the writing is pure and simple high-adventure fiction, one need only remind oneself that fiction allows for larger-than-life characters, liberal interpretations of physical laws, and more action in a single chapter than most of us will see in a lifetime. *Journal of a Combat Tanker* would be good high-adventure fiction but for one significant exception—it all actually happened just the way it is told.

In *Journal of a Combat Tanker* the author, Toby Brant, pictures for the reader a ground level, close-enough-to-smell-the-diesel account of the everyday life of the combat tanker. It is truly rare to encounter one who has seen real war from the "common soldier's" perspective who can in turn relate his experiences with any semblance of literary grace. Brant's style and use of GI jargon threads a comfortable, readable, and patently honest line between propriety and vulgarity. It is a soldier's story, one well told over beer and pretzels. It farts without apology, laughs that ancient, lusty laugh, and yet testifies to that tender sensitivity that so often is birthed as result of the pain and horror of war.

In *Journal of a Combat Tanker*, Toby Brant first poses the invitation to "put yourself in my place," and then makes it so very easy to do just that. Above all, in a market that seems to insist on making psychotics out of the Vietnam veterans, either before, during, or after, this book portrays the Vietnam experience from a wholly balanced and normal posture. It's a book by and for the normal—those who are mindful enough to be thankful for that, if for nothing else.

Captain Steve Harrison
Vietnam Veteran

ACKNOWLEDGMENTS

I WOULD LIKE TO ACKNOWLEDGE my good friend and advisor, Steve L. Harrison, for his guidance, technical assistance, and support throughout this project.

I would also like to acknowledge Missy Carey for her timely advice, and my thanks go out to Cathy Lawyer for the friendship and special skills that I would have been hardpressed to do without.

My very special thanks to all my friends and family who believed in me, but most of all to my wife, Billie Jean, for her love, support, and encouragement when I needed it most, and for making me believe in myself when my confidence might otherwise have waned.

Finally my gratitude goes out to my daughter, Nikki L. Brant, for her love and belief in her daddy's abilities.

INTRODUCTION

I HAD CONSIDERED WRITING this book for a long time before it ever began to take form. The healing process of time had to do its work before I felt I could do any justice to this story or put it in the proper perspective.

Although it has now been over fifteen years since I served in Vietnam, many of the events are still fresh in my mind as though they happened only yesterday. The names of individuals are another thing. For some reason the names of my comrades have faded quickly from my memory. I suppose this is a built-in self-protection mechanism that God has given us to shut out some of the pain and horror of war.

This book is not an attempt to write a history of the Vietnam War. It is more of a journal of impressions, anecdotes, and memories that made an imprint upon my mind in the brief time I served in Vietnam. I am not striving for accuracy so much as I am trying to convey a feeling of how it felt to be nineteen and scared and in the middle of a very unpopular war.

The events in this book are as true as my memory will allow with the passage of time. Many of the names have been changed to avoid embarrassment and to protect the privacy of certain individuals.

> There is a price which is too great to pay for peace, and that price can be put in one word. One cannot pay the price of self-respect.
>
> Woodrow Wilson
> January 8, 1918

Chapter 1

I SAT WAITING IN THE FAMILY CAR with my parents and a girl friend on a cold and dreary winter day. We were outside of the small, nondescript air terminal at Scott Air Force Base in southwestern Illinois. The snow was gently falling, and the longer we sat the more tense the atmosphere became. We were waiting for the airplane that would start me on my journey to the Republic of South Vietnam.

After a wild and woolly thirty-five-day leave, which my friends and I spent boozing it up night after night, carousing around and bar-hopping, I was as ready as I would ever be to leave for my unknown future in the war zone.

I was born and raised in the small college town of Charleston, Illinois, which is located in the east-central part of the state. Until I enlisted in the army in 1968 at the age of eighteen, I had hardly been away from home. Here I was, a year later, a buck sergeant at age nineteen and headed for Vietnam.

Everyone was trying very hard to keep their emotions in check and act like nothing was wrong. We all knew if any one of us started blubbering we all would cut loose, especially my mother as she is the most emotional and tender-hearted person in the world. I did not want to do or say anything to upset her any more than she already was.

God only knows what was going on in Dad's mind. He is a big, burly guy with a heart to match, but he normally tries not to show his emotions. Dad spent a hitch in the

Navy during World War II and he served six years in the Army following that. I am sure he had a good idea of the ordeal I would be facing in the very near future. I am not sure if I could be as brave as he was that day as he waited for his only son to board a plane for a nearly unknown country to go to war.

My girl friend Debbie held up fairly well until the very last; then she nearly became hysterical, upsetting everyone in the process. It was quite a show considering she sent me a Dear John letter after two whole months of separation from the time I left.

The time for my plane's departure had arrived. So, with lumps as big as golf balls in our throats and misty-eyed as hell, we said our goodbyes, not knowing if it would be the last time we saw one another in this world. Dad and I had decided it would be easier on Mom if she didn't have to watch the airplane fly away, so I went into the terminal alone. I waved goodbye and watched them as they drove out of sight.

As luck would have it, the air force operated about like the army does—SNAFU. My flight was delayed about four hours, so there I sat. Fortunately, on this January 13, Superbowl III was being played and they had it tuned in on the lounge television. As I now recall the New York Jets, lead by the flawless passing of Broadway Joe Namath, beat the Baltimore Colts and Johnny Unitas handily. I don't remember the final score, but then my mind wasn't on football.

When my plane finally arrived, I was glad to see I had not been bumped; I was damn tired of waiting around.

The airplane was a large converted cargo aircraft with passenger seats installed, and it was as cold as hell. We had a fairly uneventful flight to McGuire Air Force Base on the east coast. It seemed to me we were going the wrong direction to get to Vietnam, but what the hell did I know, I was only a sergeant.

The airport terminal was mass confusion with thousands of soldiers coming and going every hour. I took a taxi to Fort Dix, where I was to wait for further orders and transportation overseas. While I was there we received classes on Vietnamese customs, got vaccinated and were given all kinds of advice, most of which proved entirely useless. Most of our time was spent lying around reading comic books and playing poker. Finally, I received my travel orders and was sent back to the airport terminal at McGuire A.F.B. ready to ship out. My earlier suspicions proved to be true as far as directions go. We were now ready to go to Vietnam by way of Alaska.

There were ninety-some guys going over with me. A couple of the men had gone through the NCO Academy at Fort Knox, Kentucky with me. I was pleasantly surprised to see that we were leaving on a commercial Boeing 707 with stewardesses, hot meals and warm, comfortable seats. We took off and after only a few hours had landed in Anchorage, Alaska. I was dressed in a short-sleeved summer uniform with no coat as I was expecting to be in the tropics soon. As you can imagine, we landed in Alaska to find the temperature was twenty degrees below zero. We had a short layover while the plane was being refueled.

The cold was not really all that noticeable as we madly raced one another to the airport lounge where we all proceeded to down as many beers or double shots as we had time for, or money enough to buy. We were refueled ourselves now and ready with steady nerves and shaky legs to continue our journey.

The flight to Japan seemed to take forever. We were flying at forty thousand feet, and at that altitude you can not see much in the way of scenery. This was not the champagne flight so we had no movies or booze. The army likely sabotaged us. "We can't have the troops having fun, you know, bad for discipline!" About all we could do was sit, sleep, and bullshit with one another. We all passed along flirtatious remarks to the airline stewardesses, who in all probability had heard every line in existence from hundreds of thousands of horny, homesick GIs. It didn't stop us from trying, and they were great sports, taking everything in stride. After all, we would soon get ours.

We landed in Japan, where our aircraft blew a tire. We had a short layover while the tire was repaired and the ship was refueled again. There was time to wander around for awhile, but not much chance to soak up any local color before it was time to head out on our final leg of the trip. I could not help but notice how beautiful the night was as I viewed the lit-up cities and streets of Japan as we gently climbed into the cloudless sky.

We were now headed nonstop to Vietnam. I suppose a million thoughts must have raced through my mind at this time, but they all seemed disconnected and followed no organized pattern. I really can't remember any details of the last leg of my journey to the country that was to be my home for the next year. It seemed as though the nervous anticipation I was feeling had chased all other details from my mind.

Before I knew it, the pilot was announcing that we were over Vietnam. We all scrambled to the windows wondering with dread and excitement what this country was really like. It was still dark and we could see only a few parachute flares lighting up the night far below us. Every so often we could see a string of tracers or a stray round screaming on its way into oblivion. I soon found out this was the only way to view a war—from as far away as possible.

We were all nervous about being shelled while landing, but it came off without a hitch. As we taxied up to the tin and corrugated buildings that served as a terminal, the older hands who were serving their second tour of duty in Nam began to jabber among themselves. I am sure they were all asking themselves what the hell were they doing back in this hell hole. As the airplane hatches were opened, a hot, musty, pungent breeze gently blew in, carrying with it the smell of rotting vegetation and the humid night air, smelling as only Vietnam can smell. We were there, in the country we had worked so hard to prepare for.

Chapter 2

AMERICANS ON THE WHOLE TEND TO BE OPTIMISTIC, but I am afraid my optimism tended to fade after one look at Bien Hoa Air Force Base. Not that it was any different than any other base in Vietnam, I just had not had time to grow accustomed to the bleakness of the military bases in a war zone.

Most of these bases were supposed to be temporary, so no one went to any great pains to spruce anything up. I had arrived during the dry season and a layer of dust was on everything in sight, a condition that one soon gets used to, or at the very least you learn to tolerate it. As anyone who has ever been to Vietnam will tell you, there are only two seasons in this country: hot and dry, and hot and wet. The nights tend to get chilly—not really cold, just uncomfortable and damp. No matter what the season, you can always count on the mosquitoes to try their best to eat you alive. There was an old joke going around about a large mosquito landing on a helicopter pad and a whole ground crew running out to service and refuel it before they realized what it was. After being in the country for a while you could almost believe it.

From Bien Hoa Air Force Base we were taken by bus to the Ninetieth Replacement Center. It was in the dead of night when we were herded on board, and the ride was pretty spooky. We all felt really defenseless without any weapons at all. A person always feels a whole lot braver when he has something to defend himself with.

The bus windows were covered with a wire mesh which we were told was there to prevent any hand grenades from being thrown into the bus. This little tidbit of information did nothing to instill confidence or trust. Our nervousness amounted to naught, for we were deposited safely at the Ninetieth Replacement Center compound shortly thereafter.

We spent nearly three hours standing around, dog tired, waiting for something to happen or someone to take charge and let us know what to do. Finally, one by one our names were called out and we began receiving our issue of jungle fatigues, socks, boots, helmets, and other essential gear. At around two in the morning we were shown to a scroungy-looking barracks, called a hootch in Nam, where we could at long last lay our tired bodies down and get some long overdue sleep. Due to our excitement at being in Vietnam, sleep seemed pretty elusive until fatigue overcame us. The next morning there was not much of anything to do except wander aimlessly around the company area until my orders came down.

I think one of the things that most surprised me at first was the great number of Vietnamese civilians that were free to move around the base. It sure seemed as though security was awfully lax. I guessed that someone must know what they were doing, or at least I hoped so. Vietnamese civilians were used for any number of jobs on American bases. They mostly worked at jobs that the American soldier was loath to do, such as cleaning hootches, pulling KP and other mess hall duty. The Vietnamese did laundry, shined boots, and hauled trash in which they found many treasures the wasteful Americans threw away. The Vietnamese even burned our feces, which I guessed was about as lowly a job as there could be. They did this by removing the buckets of shit from under the latrines and pouring diesel fuel on it and burning it until there was nothing left but ashes. I doubt if the shit burners had many friends. Any of the Vietnamese that were lucky enough to land a job on an American base were fortunate indeed because they could make more money in a month than most of their countrymen could make in a year. This tended to cause their economy untold problems. As usual the American soldier tended to be recklessly generous with his money in most situations.

While I was awaiting my orders I happened to bump into an old acquaintance I knew from Fort Knox, Kentucky. I had met Dave Spence while attending the armor school at Fort Knox. This was an NCO academy more commonly and disdainfully called the "shake and bake" or the "instant NCO" program. Its purpose was to train men to become sergeants to fill a gap in the noncommissioned officers' ranks. In essence, most of us were a lot less experienced than our older, more traditionally promoted counterparts. This tended to make it a lot harder for us to gain the respect and trust of most men. In other words, we had to earn it, and rightfully so.

I didn't really know Dave all that well, but any familiar face at that point in time was like meeting a long-lost brother. Spence was every bit as thrilled to see me as I was to see him. It felt pretty darn good to find a friend among so many strangers. We quickly cemented our relationship over a few beers. He and I contemplated our upcoming assignments. We had not as yet been assigned anywhere, but we both had high hopes we might be lucky enough to be sent to the same unit or base camp. We buddied around for the next two days, trying our best to find something to do to kill time. We even volunteered to help build a new bunker. There is nothing worse than waiting around with nothing to keep you busy. When we did receive our orders, the Army, in its usual fashion, screwed things up and we were sent to totally different areas of the country. I have not seen or heard from Spence since that day. I pray to God he finished his tour of duty and made it back home in one piece as he was a real fine guy.

I was soon on the old bus again and back to the Bien Hoa air field. There, as usual, I waited and waited for a plane to take me to a place called Cu Chi, my future base camp. It seems like in the army you spend at least half your time waiting for something, whether it is meals, orders, transportation, or just some damn fool trying to make up his mind.

As I was lying on the concrete floor of the airport terminal with my head propped upon my duffle bag, I nearly freaked out. Here comes this little Vietnamese kid who walked up beside me with no britches on and takes a big, healthy shit right on the floor not five feet away. I thought to myself, *Jesus Christ, what next!* Well, mama san walked up nonchalantly as hell with a napkin, scooped up the shit just as neat as you please, and dropped it into a trash can. Then she walked away giggling her ass off. I was somewhat relieved the mess was cleaned up, but so much for trying to get comfortable. I had suddenly, from that moment on, found sleeping on airport floors to be rather distasteful.

The Vietnamese countryside is as beautiful as any country in the world and it is as varied as any country. It runs from triple-canopy jungle, mountains, swamps, flat plains, desert, rice paddies, and just about everything in between. As an amateur artist I have a fairly broad eye for beauty. But after a while it gets real hard to find beauty in anything over there when all you can see is danger lurking behind every tree and death under every bush.

My plane finally arrived and I was on my way to Cu Chi. The aircraft was a small twin-engine cargo plane, and when those pilots take off or land they do it at the steepest angle possible to avoid sniper and ground fire. If you are not used to these maneuvers it can be just a little bit disconcerting. You just know that somewhere your belly is still on the ground and your heart is in your throat. The pilots are thoroughly professional and it is pretty rare to hear of one cracking up unless it is by ground fire from unseen enemy gunners. We had no sooner landed on an airstrip that looked like a postage stamp than I was disembarked and they were back airborne and had disappeared from sight. There I stood on a dusty air strip in Cu Chi, my future home. It sure as hell didn't look like much, but I was determined to make the best of it.

Chapter 3

CU CHI IS A SMALL TOWN situated approximately thirty-five miles northwest of Saigon on Route 1. Our base camp was located just a short distance from this town and it went by the same name. The Twenty-Fifth Infantry Division was based here as a blocking force between major infiltration routes coming out of the Ho Chi Minh Trail from Cambodia toward the capital of South Vietnam, Saigon.

After leaving the plane that brought me to Cu Chi, I waited at the side of the airstrip. Shortly, a three-quarter-ton truck, driven by a spec. four, picked me up and delivered me to yet another replacement company.

I spent the rest of that day filling out paperwork, and at the end of the day I was shown to a large tent with rows of cots where I spent a restless night. The next morning, January 21, I had breakfast, then a group of Red Cross girls we called "doughnut dollies" passed out juice, and of course doughnuts, to everyone in sight.

What with all the training I had received in the States, I felt I was pretty well prepared for Vietnam. The United States Army had different ideas, however. I was about to commence a one week "in-country" training course. We were given instruction on the nature of communist weaponry being used against us. They would use everything from 122mm rockets to punji traps and every conceivable weapon in between. The Vietcong could be very ingenious when it came to utilizing any and all materials at hand to construct deadly weapons.

The Vietcong were particularly adept at constructing booby traps to injure or maim the unwary. Their booby traps took all forms. They used sharpened bamboo stakes in pits to impale their victims, much as their ancestors trapped tigers and other game. They used our dud artillery shells and unexploded bombs to make hand grenades, antipersonnel mines, and antitank mines. They did this by removing the explosives from the duds or by simply replacing the faulty detonator with one of their own manufacture and attaching a trip wire or other device to set it off. The majority of our own casualties were inflicted by booby traps. These damn things were everywhere. A man never took a step without first looking carefully, but then there were no sure ways of detecting or avoiding them.

We were shown how the Vietcong constructed tunnels for use as bomb shelters, base camps, hospitals or just plain old hiding places. I do believe the whole damn country was riddled with tunnels.

I couldn't believe it when I was told I would have to go through the C.S. gas training again. C.S. gas is a strong tear gas that makes your eyes water, your nose run, your lungs burn, and it makes your skin itch worse than a case of crabs. I had been through this same shit once in basic training, twice in advanced training, again in the NCO academy and still again while I was training recruits at Fort Knox. I can tell you I was entirely fed up with this crap. What they do is have you go into an empty building with your gas mask on, then pull the pin on a couple of gas grenades. After the C.S. gas is really thick, you are ordered to remove your gas masks. You then have to stand there until you are nearly choked half to death. You are then allowed to file out in an orderly fashion, providing you have not already expired by then.

The army in Vietnam was using the M-16 rifle at this time, and most of us had trained with the older M-14 rifle. Most of the men had more faith in the older rifle as it was considered to be more reliable and it had more stopping power. We did not have any say-so in the choice of weapons, therefore it was necessary to have instruction on the M-16 rifle. As a tanker I was not real concerned, but I did consider it prudent to learn everything I could to give myself a better chance for survival. You never know.

I was assigned to a tank outfit at the end of the week. After being driven to the company area I reported for duty to Company A, Second Battalion of the Thirty-Fourth Armored Regiment. The Thirty-Fourth was split up among several infantry divisions in Vietnam to provide support for the foot soldier and the mechanized infantry units. A Company was assigned to the Twenty-Fifth Infantry Division, "Tropical Lightning."

After checking in at the Company Commander's office I was issued a .45 caliber automatic pistol and an M-16 rifle for my personal weapons. I felt a lot safer being armed. Next I was shown to my living quarters. This was a small hootch that housed around eight men whenever they were in base camp. The supply sergeant, an older career man, introduced me to the first platoon sergeant. Sergeant Domingo seemed to be a decent sort of guy and I was to be assigned to his tank as a gunner. In Vietnam we did not use gunners to fire the tank weapons. The tank commander could fire the tank guns from his position just as well, so he usually did just that. The gunner rode the bustle rack on the back of the turret with a rifle or machine gun and watched out for his ass. With all the tunnels and spider holes in Nam this was a very prudent measure. It was not unusual for a sniper to pop out of a hole after a tank had gone by and put an RPG (rocket-propelled grenade) through the engine compartment or fuel tank which would promptly blow you all to hell.

Sergeant Domingo soon introduced me to Junior Underwood, his driver, and Bill Butters, the loader. Junior was a cocky, good-natured kid, but he had an irritating habit of calling everybody a fool, such as "What are you doing, fool?" or "Hi, fool." I learned he did not mean anything by it and I let it go in one ear and out the other. I guess he thought it sounded cool or something. Of necessity, a tank crew has to be close and it has to be able to operate as a unit, so the last thing you need is friction among yourselves.

Bill Butters was an easygoing Texan who hardly ever got excited about anything. I liked Bill right off and we got along real well together. Bill was twenty-five or twenty-six years old and a private first class. I was only nineteen and a buck sergeant. Twenty-six was considered somewhat old for the average soldier in Vietnam. The average age was nineteen to twenty. We tended to balance each other out pretty well. Whenever Bill gave me any advice I always listened because he had been in the country longer than me and I respected him. To hell with the differences in rank, that didn't cut much ice over there and I wanted to stay alive. I was more than willing to take any good advice that came my way if I thought it would help me in any way.

We used the M-48–A3 tank in Vietnam. It was an older tank that originally had a gasoline engine, but it had been modified to use the newer and less volatile diesel engine. A combat loaded M-48 weighed approximately fifty-three tons and it carried a ninety-millimeter main gun. It also mounted an M-73, 7.62 coaxial machine gun mounted in the turret. Up above we carried two big fifty-caliber machine guns, one for the tank commander and an extra one mounted in front of the loader hatch. The tank commander's fifty was designed to be mounted in the cupola, but there was only room to store a hundred rounds of ammunition mounted inside. We mounted the T.C.'s fifty above the cupola so we could carry over three hundred rounds of ready ammunition and we could see better when we fired it. As to other weapons, we used anything we could beg, borrow or steal, anything to give us the edge. Our tank crew had in its possession three M-16 rifles, three .45 pistols, one M-79 grenade launcher, one M-60 light machine gun, one .45 caliber submachine gun (called a grease gun), one 12-gauge pump shotgun, three machetes, a knife, and two cases of hand grenades. We also had ammunition for everything. In other words, we were loaded for bear!

After getting a look at the tank that I was to be crewing in, I was appalled. That thing was filthy. I wasn't worried about the appearance at all, but the main gun didn't look like it had ever been cleaned. So, one of the first things I did was to tear down the breech of the cannon and clean it thoroughly. Bill Butters and I then swabbed the gun tube out. Bill had always been good about cleaning the fifties and other weapons, but he had trained as an infantryman and he had no knowledge of how to take apart a ninety-millimeter tank gun and put it back together. I guess Sergeant Domingo was either too busy or too lazy to do it himself. At any rate, after the job was done I felt a lot safer.

Most of the first week that I was with the Thirty-Fourth was spent in getting to know everyone. We drank beer, worked on the tank, or cleaned weapons. A lot of the men outside of my own tank crew were hard to get to know. They were a tried and true fraternity of men who knew what the hell was going on and I was still just "a cherry." This meant that I had not proved myself under fire and was still an unknown factor. These men had to know that I would be reliable when the heat was on before I could ever be fully accepted.

This was still a big question in my own mind: *How will I react under fire?* You always wonder until it actually happens. In most cases I think a person is more afraid of showing fear in front of his comrades than he is of dying. Well, I would have my turn soon enough, and so far I was not overly anxious, but I was getting a bit curious. What is that about the cat and curiosity? I sure as hell wasn't that curious.

Chapter 4

SERGEANT DOMINGO INFORMED ME and the rest of the crew that the First Platoon was to go on a mine sweep that morning. At last, after all the waiting and training, I was finally going to get to do something useful. This operation was just a routine armored patrol. Every morning at sunrise our company was required to send a detachment of tanks to run a mine sweep. This amounted to accompanying an engineer unit with metal detectors down Highway 8 Alpha. This duty had to performed every morning before opening the roads to traffic. It was a whole lot safer to send a fifty-three-ton tank down these roads than any other vehicle, just in case the engineers happened to miss a mine. Normally if a tank hit a mine a road wheel or two might be blown off, or the track might be broken, but it was very rare to hit a mine big enough to cause casualties to the crew.

I was all eyes as I took in the strange countryside. It sure was nothing like Illinois. The kids were always out in force when the tankers came by. The little fellas were always right there waiting for a handout. We always had candy left over from S.P. packages that we threw to the kids as we went by, and they knew it. An S.P. pack is a box of goodies handed out to the troops in the field. It contained cigarettes, pens, writing paper, candy and other assorted items to supplement our normal rations. I have seen little guys that were just barely old enough to walk out on the roadside yelling, "Chop-chop, chop-chop," meaning food, at the top of their little lungs. It would really grab at your heart strings. Of course, there were the elderly and disabled begging for food, too. They didn't get quite as much sympathy as the little ones. The Vietnamese government didn't have much of a public aid system. In the few instances they attempted to give aid to the needy, their government officials proved to be so corrupt that only they reaped the benefits of this so-called aid.

Most of our mine sweeps went without incident and only rarely did we hit a mine or receive any sniper fire during daylight patrols. There were times when after the roads were cleared the Vietcong would sneak out during a lull in traffic and replant a mine. If a truck happened to hit one it would naturally be blown to smithereens. You could see these derelicts alongside any road in Vietnam. nam.

The Vietnamese didn't have many cars or trucks, but they had thousands of small Hondas. These small motor bikes seemed to be the main mode of transportation, other than walking or using a bicycle. The Lambretta was the most common vehicle for carrying commodities and people. The Lambretta was a three-wheeled truck that reminded me of the old Cushman motor scooter, only it had a bed on the back. The Vietnamese would load these things down till you swore they would collapse, then they would load it some more and go *putt-putt-putting* on down the road.

The villages were pretty primitive by our standards. The average Vietnamese hootch had only two or three rooms. They were constructed using bamboo and mud for the walls and the roof was bamboo poles thatched with rice straw or elephant grass. Some of the more enterprising families managed to acquire corrugated tin for their roofs and side walls. The Vietnamese always had a small bunker dug beneath their homes for obvious reasons. The mama san nearly always cooked outside over an open fire in good weather. When it was raining, she would cook under a lean-to type of shelter.

While driving through a village you could always count on seeing numerous merchants hawking their wares. Naturally the most popular merchandise with the GIs was ice, Coke, beer, whiskey, and women, not necessarily in that order. I had heard how beautiful the Saigon prostitutes were, but where I was they looked pretty rough . . . at least at first they did. Just about any village on the main routes had its pimps and whores lined up outside their various abodes and places of business. They would make lewd gestures and yell out, "Hey, GI, you want boom boom? Me numba one lay, GI!" They were fine if you were partial to VD.

The area I was in was mostly flatlands. This area was called the Central Plains. Upon these lands were constructed hundreds of rice paddies surrounded by earthen dikes. In the dry season the paddies were mostly bone dry, and tanks could maneuver quite easily. It was very bumpy and rough going over the dikes. Papa san was not too thrilled about having his dikes mashed down, either. In the wet season or monsoon weather the armored outfits were pretty much confined to the hard roads and base camps.

After making a few routine mine sweeps I went on my first thunder run. After dark in Vietnam, Charlie reigned supreme. The Americans would generally dig in for the night and take stationary positions. The only exception to this rule was an occasional patrol or night ambush. Every once in a while the tanks and personnel carriers were sent out on the highways after dark just to throw Charlie off balance and to help prevent him from planting more mines. We would take off from base camp at full speed down Highway 1 and would go as far as Phu Cong on the Saigon River east of Cu Chi. We would then turn around and roar on back to base camp. The thunder runs were pretty hairy at times. One never knew if you would run into a trap or an ambush. It was not very hard for the Vietcong to put an antitank round through your vehicle. He would then disappear into the night just as quickly as if he were never there.

At the village of Phu Cong there was a large bridge where Highway 1 crossed the Saigon River. Highway 1 was the most important supply route in this area and it had to be kept open. Once a month our platoon had to furnish two or three tanks for a night to guard the bridge against saboteurs. A tank had gone to the bottom of the river not long before I came into Vietnam. The Vietcong had swum underneath the bridge and blown it up while a tank was sitting on the middle span. This did not happen after the men started throwing concussion grenades into the water at regular intervals. The grenades tended to burst the eardrums of anyone swimming underwater close to the bridge. This had happenedd in the case of a South Vietnamese navy diver who was checking the structure out for enemy charges. Some fool threw a grenade in the water unaware of the fact that one of our guys was down there.

We really liked the outpost job on the bridge because it was pretty cushy duty compared to other things. It sure beat being in the bush. A family of Vietnamese ran a small bar out of their house right beside the bridge. When we weren't on guard duty Bill Butters and I would go down and drink beer. We would bullshit with mama san and watch television with the little kids. The program was always in Vietnamese so we didn't have any idea what was being said. Even so we would laugh right along with everyone else to be polite. We didn't want to hurt their feelings after accepting their hospitality. Sometimes papa san would get out his guitar and play us a few tunes. We didn't recognize any of the songs, but when you get drunk to a certain point it doesn't matter what songs are being played.

The Vietnamese had a popular beer called 33. A lot of the guys didn't like it at all, but to me it tasted just like a good home brew with a nice yeasty sort of flavor. If you were not used to the local beer you could get in bad trouble. Many a soldier got the screaming shits and a bellyache the next morning. I must have had a good constitution.

Charlie Cong always seemed to have a knack for attacking when it was my turn to sleep. The only trouble we ever had at the bridge was a sniper who would take a few pot shots, and then slip away. The little bastard never hit anything to my knowledge; he just managed to rouse everyone up and ruin a good night's sleep.

The first time I ever saw a dead body it sobered me considerably. We were making a mine sweep down Highway 1 when Butters yelled to me, "Hey, Toby, look at that." We were just coming into a village east of Cu Chi and there was an ARVN (South Vietnamese Army) compound at the edge of the village. Bill said, "They got a body count!" I thought, *What in the hell is a body count?* I guess I had visions of a bunch of bodies piled up like cordwood or something. I looked up ahead and I could see civilians and ARVN soldiers milling around at the side of the road. Everyone looked like they were as proud as punch. As we got closer, I could then see a human form lying on the shoulder of the road. He was a young Vietnamese male, dressed in black pajamas. I guarantee you, he was dead as hell. His side was half blown away with his guts hanging out, and there were several bullet holes in him. Now, I had seen dead bodies before, but never outside of a funeral home. This dude looked real gruesome to me, and I am sure I looked just a little bit pale even though I tried not to show it. I felt a slight sinking feeling in the pit of my stomach. Bill and everyone else felt real happy about the situation, but I wasn't quite in the mood to celebrate. I thought to myself, *Jesus Christ, these motherfuckers are really playing for keeps*! It had finally soaked in—I might not make it of here alive. Later on, as I got used to things, I would be just as happy as everyone else if we got a body count. That always meant there was one less VC to shoot at me or my buddies.

Chapter 5

I WAS GETTING SETTLED IN as part of the crew by now and I was due to go on my first operation in the bush. Most of our time was occupied by going on patrols or patching up the tanks afterwards. All the heat and dust of Vietnam makes for considerable wear and tear on engines and bearings. That is why we spent as much time pulling maintenance as we did patrolling.

On this particular patrol we were going out north of the base camp. The area north of Cu Chi is a rough, barren, and a mostly uninhabited stretch of land all the way to the Saigon River, about ten miles away. Five tanks and five personnel carriers with infantrymen would make up a typical armored patrol. We would take off cross-country and see if we could stir up any activity from the Vietcong or VC sympathizers.

If we ran across any tunnels, the normal procedure would be to throw a grenade in it and drive on, unless we got a secondary explosion. If that happened, we would check it out. There were just too many tunnels and holes to check out each and every one of them.

We searched and drove for hours at a time with the hot, blistering sun bearing down. The heat from the engine, a big V-12 diesel, and the sun reflecting off the steel hull of the tank would make for a pretty hot day.

Most patrols were boring as hell, but there was always an element of danger and an offhand chance we could be attacked. This time we didn't run into any trouble, with the exception of hitting an ant tree. There were large red ants in Vietnam that could bite like hell. For some odd reason, they liked to climb up young trees and hang there in clusters. They would wait in ambush for an unsuspecting vehicle such as a tank to come along. When we hit this little tree full of ants they would fall off all over our tank and us. There was only one thing to do, and that was to stop the tank and scramble like hell for a broom and start sweeping them off before the little bastards ate you alive. After brooming down the tank as best we could, we would then break out the insect spray and go over every crack and crevice we could find. It was impossible to get them all without getting bitten in several places.

As we went on a sweep through hostile territory we would move in a wedge or V formation. When the foliage would get real thick the infantry would dismount and check the area ahead for hidden ambushes. As the sun started setting we would start looking for a halfway clear area to set up a night perimeter. Once a suitable area had been selected we would circle our vehicles, much the same as the wagon trains of old. Five tanks and five personnel carriers would be facing out, with a tank, PC, tank, PC, et cetera, until we had a complete circle. This makes for a pretty formidable fort for the night.

Now, when you are in a tank there is no way in the world you can be quiet. The hydraulic pump kicks on and off every fifteen minutes making a loud, high-pitched whine, and you have to start the main engine periodically to ensure the batteries stay charged. You also have to remember that a tank is a mighty big piece of equipment to hide behind a bush. With a tank you have a tremendous amount of firepower to call upon, but you also make one hell of a big target. All in all, there is just no point in trying to be sneaky. Even in the field we would play our transistor radios on low volume, unless we really expected to get hit. This would naturally freak out any straight-leg infantry units working with us. We noisy-assed tankers would really blow their minds. We figured, "Hell, Charlie knows where we are, so why worry about it." About the only thing we could do was to try and out gun the VC. We usually did just that.

A tank will normally have a four-man crew, although we could get by with three men. We would take two-hour shifts on guard duty at night. Everyone took a turn. Every half-hour we would check in with our platoon leader, Lieutenant Solars, on the radio to make sure no one was sleeping. Men have been known to get their heads knocked half-off by falling asleep on guard duty. I am not talking about the enemy doing it either. You would not keep friends very long if you happened to be foolish enough to go to sleep and leave them unprotected. We were dog tired all of the time. There were times when we were so tired it would get darn rough staying awake, but the thought of a VC slipping up and cutting your throat was enough to dispel any thought of an untimely nap.

At home a person doesn't think much about the moon, except as something to kiss under. In Vietnam it was a whole different story. We would follow that old moon through all its phases, and dread it like hell when he didn't show his face. On an overcast night with no moon it gets so dark you can't see your hand in front of your face. That is no exaggeration, either. It's scary as hell when you know a Vietcong can walk right up to one of those noisy-assed tanks in the dark and you can't see him. Not even a starlight scope (a night-vision device) is any good on a really black night. We had infrared search lights, but Charlie was known to have infrared devices, too, so we didn't want to furnish him with a clear target to home in on with his mortars.

We all slept with a rifle or a pistol, so if a person

went to wake up someone he would just touch them on the toe. Any other approach could get him either clubbed or shot. It is really amazing how one's senses become attuned to every little sound. I'm a heavy sleeper, but in Vietnam I could be asleep and hear the grass move as someone walked by. Fear does that to you.

That first night in the bush I got the surprise of my life. As I was straining my eyes into the dark I heard a high-pitched voice off in the distance yell, "Fuck you!" Well, that sent a chill down my spine. I woke up Bill Butters and told him to listen. Pretty soon, here it comes again. Bill started to laugh a little bit, and then he told me that it was just a "fuck you" lizard. I just couldn't believe a little lizard could be so uncouth. I never did know the proper name of that little reptile, but to me it will always be a "fuck you" lizard for as long as I live.

Whenever we would attempt to sleep the mosquitoes would attack with a vengeance. I still think they were working for the other side. They would even bite right through your jungle fatigues. About the only way of avoiding them was to douse yourself with mosquito repellent and cover your whole body, head and all, with a blanket.

The only blanket we used in Nam was a camouflaged, lightweight nylon cover called a poncho liner. The poncho liners were very serviceable and easy to store away. They could be compressed down to the size of a cigar box when they were folded tight.

Our meals in the boonies were usually the old tried and true C rations. We would carry hot sauce on the tank to help vary the monotony of them, but nothing helped much. We would carry a demolition pouch full of C-4 explosives to cook with. All a soldier had to do was pinch off a little piece of C-4 and put it under his C rations and light it. That stuff would burn a pretty blue flame and it would heat better than Sterno. You just didn't ever want to make the mistake of stamping out your cook fire. That would be a good way to lose a foot. The C-4 also came in handy for blowing foxholes so you didn't have to dig so hard, and we also used it to set dry brush on fire as we moved through an area.

One of the nice things about being on a tank is that you can carry extra C rations and plenty of beer with you. We always had a better choice of C rations, as we carried four or five cases with us most of the time. We would eat what we wanted and trade for other rations with what we didn't like. If the particular rations were some that nobody wanted we would trade them to the Vietnamese for cheap whiskey or ice to cool our beer. Some of the more enterprising men supplemented their rations with Vienna sausages, Spam, and sardines (more commonly known as "canned pussy" in Nam).

Butters and I would often spell the driver for awhile when on an operation. The tracks of a tank can kick up more dust than you can imagine and the driver always gets the worst of it. Junior Underwood really appreciated a break now and then so he could come up on top and get a little fresh air.

The next day as I was giving Junior a breather I was tooling along just fine when a funny looking little creature landed at my feet in the driver's compartment. I asked over the intercom, "Hey, does anyone know what a scorpion looks like?" It so happened that no one did. "Well," I yelled, "I think I have one in here with me!" I stopped and dis-assed that tank in a big hurry. I then grabbed a stick and did the little bugger in. I got back in the driver's hatch and damned if I didn't find another one. I made record time stopping the tank and killed him, too. It turned out that they were scorpions, so I didn't feel so foolish for abandoning my duty so abruptly. After the scorpion episode everything else went smoothly. We returned to base camp that afternoon for a cold beer, a cold shower, and a good night's sleep.

I hadn't seen any action other than battling ants, mosquitoes, and scorpions, plus a near-verbal battle with a lizard, but I did have a patrol under my belt and I felt a little more like one of the team.

Chapter 6

I HAD BEEN WITH MY UNIT going on four weeks and had received no major complaints, and I had made only a few minor mistakes. Everything was going well, except that I was not too impressed with Sergeant Domingo. He was a good enough soldier, but he was always bitching about little things that didn't amount to a damn. I just went ahead, did my job and ignored his crummy disposition like everyone else.

The First and Second tank platoons had just been ordered out on a search-and-destroy mission. It was rare for two platoons of tanks to go out together, and a large detachment of infantry was to work with us on this mission, so we knew that this must be something big. We were to go against a small hamlet near Dau Tieng. According to intelligence reports, this hamlet had been a Vietcong stronghold for quite some time and they wanted it cleaned out.

We readied our tanks and left early in the morning in order to give us plenty of daylight to get our job done and get out before dark. As we approached the hamlet, civilians began fleeing their homes. This was a common occurrance whenever the VC were in an area we were approaching. The innocent villagers nearly always evacuated an area that they figured was unsafe or if a skirmish was imminent. We checked their identification as they drew near so we could weed out any Vietcong trying to escape. We generally assumed that anyone not leaving the area must be the enemy, as the friendlies and noncombatants were free to go. This was about the only method we had of distinguishing the enemy.

The tanks in our unit surrounded the hamlet on three sides as Huey gunships covered the remaining avenue of escape from the air. As soon as everyone was in position, the infantry units carefully moved forward to check the hamlet for signs of enemy activity. No sooner had they begun to close in on the hamlet than the Vietcong commenced firing with automatic weapons. The United States Army always tried to avoid unnecessary casualties whenever it was at all possible, and the ground pounders were pulled back out of range. Once they were clear, our tanks and personnel carriers opened fire with everything we had. We fired cannons and machine guns into that hamlet for over five minutes. Artillery had been called in also, and we really gave them hell. If you can imagine ten cannons and thirty or more fifty caliber machine guns, all firing at you at point-blank range, along with artillery raining down, then you can guess how anybody left in that hamlet might have felt. We nearly leveled the whole place in a span of minutes. When the infantry started back again, they took only very light fire. The enemy resistance had faded to almost nothing.

Fortunately the infantry units were able to investigate the hamlet and mop up with few or no casualties to themselves. This type of softening up was not always that effective. I have to admit, I enjoyed the experience immensely. Sure, some innocent people may have lost their homes, but they should not have sheltered the Vietcong. We figured, to hell with them. We were not about to risk American lives to save a few hootches belonging to some very suspicious Vietnamese. I know this may sound pretty cruel to the uninitiated, but no one ever said war was fair.

I don't know what the exact body count came to that day. All I know is that it was enough to deem the operation a success. One tanker even blew a water buffalo in two with a well-placed shot from a ninety-millimeter tank round. The brass really frowned upon these antics, but, what the hell, it was good for our morale. We moved around the area on a sweep through the brush hoping to find more VC or NVA (North Vietnamese Army regulars), but we made no more contact that day.

We left the immediate region and found a clear spot to set up a night perimeter. After we circled the tanks, we set up our trip flares, concertina wire, and RPG screen. The RPG (rocket propelled grenade) screen was just a piece of storm fence set up in front of our tanks. It would cause an RPG to detonate before it hit the tank and us. The screen was simple, but effective.

We now sat back and watched for our huge resupply choppers to fly in and bring us ammuntion to replenish our depleted stocks. These big Chinook helicopters we fondly called "jolly green giants," or, as a play on its name, "shit hooks." These big helicopters would lower a sling full of ammunition, along with a two-wheeled tanker trailer of diesel fuel to fill our thirsty V-12 diesel-guzzling tanks to the max. Our water supply was also replenished in the same manner.

If we wished to take a bath while in the field we would fill a five-gallon water can, and one man standing on the tank would pour water over the other man on the ground. The man on the ground would then hurriedly soap down and then the man up top would pour the rest of the water on him and rinse him off. We would take turns until everyone in our crew achieved a semblance of cleanliness. At least we could stand the smell of each other for a while longer. I always had the fear we would get mortared about the time I got jay-ass naked, but it never happened, thank goodness!

As darkness fell it was time for guard duty, or to grab what little sleep we could before some son of a bitch decided to wake us up again. If any letter writing was to take place it nearly always happened after dark inside the tank, under a very, very dim light. I wrote many letters in this manner, but I was always behind in answering my mail. I tried my very best to always reply to the letters I received, because it was always nice to hear from someone back home in the world. I don't suppose there is a lonelier feeling in the world than to come back empty-handed from mail call.

As we settled in for the night, a VC mortar team decided to keep us on our toes. Someone heard the dreaded, hollow-sounding "thump" of a mortar round leaving its tube and yelled, "Incoming!" We dove for cover and waited for the shells to fall. That just has to be the scariest, most nerve-wracking feeling in the world, knowing those damn mortar shells are on the way but not being able to hear them until they explode. You always feel like those suckers are going to drop right in your hip pocket. Fortunately, Charlie fired only three rounds and they all missed their target. No one spotted any muzzle flashes before he quit, so we didn't bother to return fire. There is no sense in wasting ammunition by blasting away at the darkness. We didn't get any more hostile fire for the rest of that night, so most of us managed to grab enough shut-eye to keep us going the following day.

Come morning we packed everthing up and resumed our sweeping operation. We must have covered fifteen or twenty square miles that day, and accomplished exactly nothing. We were ready to call it a day so we could head back to base camp and pull some much overdue maintenance on our vehicles. As we were getting close to friendly territory we heard a loud explosion. We all ducked our heads, thinking we were receiving incoming fire of some kind. It was soon apparent that our tank had hit a mine. The left track had been blown in two, and it quickly spun off the drive sprocket. This was not a large mine, for all it did was break the track. Luckily it had not blown off any road wheels or damaged the suspension, but we now had the unwelcome task of repairing the track. We always carried spare track blocks and all of the necessary tools to fix a broken track, but it sure was a royal pain in the ass to mess with in that hot tropical sun. No one had been injured, so we were all thankful of that. With that thought in mind, Sergeant Domingo, Underwood, Butters and myself set to work. The other tanks positioned themselves to provide security for us while we worked. The whole crew pitched in with enthusiasm. No one liked the idea of being a sitting duck in a disabled tank. It didn't take any prodding to work hard and fast to get our butts moving out of there. We were ready to get back into base camp where we knew that lots of cold beer awaited us. Within an hour everything was reassembled and we were ready to roll.

This was now the first week in February and I was no longer considered a cherry. Thank goodness! I admittedly had not seen too much action yet, but it was enough to relieve me of my green-assed rookie status. I could now be considered a veteran.

Chapter 7

EVERYONE IN VIETNAM WAS STARTING to get a little worried. The Chinese New Year, called Tet, was drawing near. It had seemed abnormally quiet in recent days, and we were filled with anxiety. It was too quiet. We were getting jumpy because we figured Charlie was building up for a large offensive. If the 1968 Tet Offensive was any indication of what to expect, we could have our hands full.

Junior Underwood had just left for a week of in-country R and R at Vung Tau. We knew exactly what he would be up to. No doubt he was trying to consume all of the availiable booze and ravage every woman in sight. Vung Tau was a popular R and R site in Vietnam because of the availability of all sorts of entertainment to please a lonely soldier away from home.

We had a new driver on the tank as a temporary replacement for Junior. Charlie Davis was a black dude with a bizarre sense of humor. We never knew what he was going to pull. As he was driving the tank toward Checkpoint Five, a small village on the way to Phu Cong, Charlie started yelling about something. I looked all around for fear he had spotted some kind of ambush. He was talking so fast I couldn't understand exactly what he was saying. He finally slowed down and said, "Look over there, Sarge; you see him?" I said, "What in the hell are you talking about, Charlie?" He said, "Over to the right, there's a soul gook!" I said, "What!" Charlie said, "There's a soul gook over there."

I looked over to where he had indicated and saw a little kid that was half Vietnamese and half black. Charlie stated firmly, "That little mutha is a gook but he has definitely got soul." I said, "Charlie, you crazy bastard, I thought we were being attacked or something. Will you can that bullshit!" Everyone had a good laugh when we realized that there was no danger.

We began throwing candy to the kids in this small village when we started to come up on a particular hootch. I had had my eye on this place for quite a while. Every time the kids from this hootch ran out to get their candy an ugly hag (whom I took to be their mother) would run out, slap the kids down, and take away all of their candy. That didn't go over too well with me or the crew, as we figured she was selling the candy on the black market. As we approached the hootch I grabbed a handful of candy with my left hand, and a brand-new bar of Lifebuoy soap in my right hand. I threw the candy out, and sure enough, here she came. I let fly with that brand-new and very hard bar of soap while blowing by at thirty miles per hour. Catfish Hunter could have done no better. I hit her right between the eyes. She did a perfect back flip and landed on her ass. I looked back and she was still lying there yelling her lungs out. I'm sure she was giving me a good cussing out. I just couldn't understand how she stayed conscious. I never once saw her take candy away from the little kids after that. That incident was the only thing approaching an atrocity I ever committed.

We drove on down the road toward Phu Cong. It was our turn to guard the bridge again. This was the closest thing to an R and R that Butters and I had seen so far, and we were looking forward to it. We parked our tank at the south end of the bridge in our usual spot. Once everything was secure, Bill grabbed some C rations and cigarettes off the tank and left. A short time later he returned, proudly holding a bottle of whiskey aloft. He had been doing a little horse trading with the Vietnamese. The brand name on the bottle was 45, and it had a kick like a .45. We put the bottle away until after dark so some greedy officer wouldn't try to confiscate it. I went down to the river with a couple of .45 automatics and did a little target shooting to kill time. I was standing on an old barge with a tin roof when I started blasting away at some tin cans. The noise really reverberated, and my ears were ringing like a cathedral on Sunday. That was about what I deserved for showing off my two-gun style.

I walked back up to the tank to discover Bill had come through again. He and the guys were building a tent, with a poncho liner, in front of the tank. Inside there were three girls. They were not too good looking, but I had seen worse. I didn't think I wanted any part of them because of the way VD ran rampant in Nam; and besides, I was nearly broke.

It was getting dark, so Butters and I broke out the whiskey. We had nothing to use for a chaser so we rummaged around in our C rations till we found some peaches and fruit cocktail. We punched a couple of holes in the cans and poured in the whiskey. We then drank out of the cans. When they ran dry we would refill them and pass them around again. Bill and I couldn't quite decide what that 45 whiskey tasted like, but we guessed it must have been a cross between scotch, gin, and kerosene. It was not very good, but it sure as hell was potent. After drinking for an hour or two those girls started to look a whole lot prettier. I only had five dollars and that was the going rate. I didn't want to leave myself totally broke, so I removed two dollars from my billfold and hid it in the tank. I went into the improvised brothel at the front of the tank and said, "How much, Mama san?" She said, "Five dollar, GI." I held out my billfold and told her, "Mama san, I only got three dollar!" She looked inside the wallet and said, "Oh, okay. One time, three dollar." Well, about five seconds later it was all over and Mama san wouldn't allow any freebies. The whiskey was really working now and I felt great.

Ten minutes later we heard a loud explosion, but we didn't worry too much about it till a soldier came up from the river's edge and told us a man had just blown his hand off. He had been throwing C-4 in the river when a charge he was about to throw blew up in his hand. The fuse had burned down prematurely and he couldn't get rid of it quick enough. That incident threw a pall of gloom over our little party. Even though we didn't know the guy, we felt really bad about him getting hurt. I suppose something like that always reminds us of our own mortality. A chopper was called and the man was medivac'd to the nearest hospital.

We went on over to Papa san's bar and drank a couple of beers. I was totally broke by then, so we went on back to the tank and polished off the rest of our rotgut whiskey. We then ate the peaches and fruit cocktail. Waste not, want not!

The rest of the night was quiet, so we slept like the dead between pulling guard duty. That next morning we were feeling rough as hell. You talk about hangovers, our heads were as big as balloons. We were now faced with the problem of getting rid of those whores who were sleeping under our tank. They didn't look near as good in the light of day. We would be in bad trouble if the commanding officer found out what we had been up to. Some South Vietnamese soldiers saved the day for us. They had a guard post next to where we spent the night, so we were really happy when they took those gals off our hands. Not ten minutes later this major came by checking everything out. If he noticed our red, bloodshot eyes, he didn't let on. He did ask us to pull the air cleaners from the tank. We pulled them out and proceeded to catch hell for not cleaning them more often. There must have been close to a pound of dust in each one. It was time for us to leave and we were more than ready by this time. We had gotten by with an awful lot of bullshit without getting caught and considered ourselves quite fortunate.

Chapter 8

JUNIOR UNDERWOOD WAS NOW BACK WITH US, none the worse for wear and tear. He had had a real fine time on his quick leave to Vung Tau. Naturally, Junior had some neat tales about his escapades back in civilization, but I won't embarrass him by relating them here.

We were back to patrolling the boondocks now, and it was still disturbingly quiet. As we moved through the rural areas we would sometimes luck out on resupply. As a morale builder, the cooks would fix a hot meal back in base camp, put it in insulated containers, and ship the hot food to us with the resupply choppers. When lunch time came around we would set up a perimeter, just like we did at night. The only drawback to getting hot meals in the field was when those big shit hooks took off. They always managed to time it right after we started to eat. Those suckers would crank up their big rotors and whip dust, chaff, and rice straw around in their minature hurricanes. It seemed as though most of it landed right smack in the middle of our plates. We then had the task of picking out the dirt and debris and straining out the sand with our teeth. It was still quite a treat after being on a steady diet of C rations.

As we passed a small, isolated village, a couple of young kids started running alongside our tanks. I couldn't figure out what they were up to until they got a little closer. They had taken a bunch of old brass shell casings and made rings out of them. They were trading their handicrafts for food or money. They made quite a haul for themselves before we got out of sight.

One thing I noticed whenever we asked any civilians if they had seen any Vietcong in their area was that we always got the same old answer: "No VC." To hear them tell it, there were never any VC around. I couldn't much blame them. Most of the people were innocent peasant farmers who just wanted to be left alone by both sides. If the Vietcong caught them giving any information to the Americans or South Vietnamese they would exact harsh reprisals on the people. Our news agencies in the United States never reported the atrocities committed by the North Vietnamese or the Vietcong. But let one American serviceman screw up, and the whole damn world would know about it the next morning. I'm not saying I condone the atrocities; I just feel our side got the shaft when it came to uncovering any dirt.

We had just finished our noon meal when an emergency call came over the radio. A long-range reconnaissance patrol (LRRP, phoneticized "Lurp") had gotten itself into some kind of trouble. They were only a mile or two away from us so we cranked up our engines and away we went. It looked and felt just like a cavalry charge right out of a John Wayne movie. We had those tanks fairly flying over the rough terrain and we could soon hear the firing up ahead. This Lurp team was pinned down in a bomb crater by the Vietcong when we came over the hill. Our tank pulled right up to the crater and we opened fire into the jungle. The patrol scurried onto the tank and we moved back away from the tree line. The Vietcong must have hauled ass as soon as we showed up, for they hardly fired a shot after we arrived. I am sure it must have been a hell of a shock for them to see our tanks charging toward their position. The men in the Lurp team were sure grateful to see us. Fortunately we had made good time in getting there and none of them were injured. The radio operator had taken the only casualty; his antenna had nearly been shot in half as it was sticking in the air. We arranged to have a chopper pick them up, and in a few minutes they were safely on their way with nothing hurt but their egos.

After the Lurp team left us we continued on our patrol. I had brought along a couple of phosphorus grenades that I picked up at our ammo dump back in Cu Chi and I was just dying to try them out. As we came up on an isolated hootch I pitched one of those grenades into some nearby brush. It went off and sprayed red hot phosphorus all over the place. The brush caught fire and we waited to see if anyone would come out. No one did, but we could see sudden flareups of fire now and again. The Chinese explosives the Vietcong used in their booby traps must have been awfully similar to our C-4. We could see several places where it blazed up as it caught fire. That brushy area must have been full of booby traps. We didn't find anything else, so we moved on.

A little further along in our patrol we found what looked like a freshly-dug grave. I reported it to Lieutenant Solars and he had us set up a perimeter for protection while the infantry dismounted and investigated my find. This may sound a little morbid, but the Vietcong often hid caches of arms and munitions in such places. The only way to find out for sure was to dig it up and see. The infantry soldiers working with us proceeded to dig up the grave. They worked away and pretty soon they came to a body. We were all watching with a morbid curiosity when an infantryman reached down and lifted this corpse's hand and began shaking it. It was comical as hell. This crazy bastard was saying, "Hiya, Charlie, how ya doing down there?" I didn't know whether to get sick or laugh. He had found the body of a NVA in uniform. They found two more bodies beneath that one. I was sitting on the tank eating a can of C rations, taking this all in, when the wind changed direction. Looking at a dead gook didn't affect my appetite one damn bit; but when I got a whiff of him I nearly gagged. That old boy was really ripe, and I suddenly lost any notion of being hungry. The last body they pulled out was all wrapped up in a rubber poncho and he looked to be a North Vietnamese officer. He was larger and better dressed than the other two, and someone had taken the pains to wrap him up nice and neat. That hadn't been done to the other bodies, so we figured he must have been a little more important. We didn't find any hidden weapons, so we started to leave. A Spec four with the infantry was pretty upset because no one bothered to rebury the corpses. We said, "To hell with it. They stink, it's hot as hell, and besides we want Charlie to feel as though he's not safe anywhere, not even in his grave." So we left them.

Not too far from the grave site we came onto a large hidden supply of rice. The rice had been sacked up in one hundred pound bags. On the outside of each bag, printed in large letters, it said, "Houston, Texas, product of USA." This find was really upsetting. Here we were in Vietnam busting our ass, and some fat cat back in the States was selling the VC rice and getting rich from our miseries. We were having a hard enough time justifying this war in our minds without some backstabbing son of a bitch at home making things worse. We knew all about the peace movement and demonstrations at home, and at the time most of us just felt betrayed by it all. We poured diesel fuel on the rice and set it on fire. There was over a thousand pounds of rice the Vietcong would never eat.

That night we would be sleeping in at fire support

base Crockett and we would be able to rest a little easier. As we came up the main trail into the fire support base we started to relax and loosen up a little bit. However, just as we got even with the big guns of the artillery they must have gotten a fire mission, because they opened up with a fury, right over our heads. Everyone in that column, including myself, was hitting the deck and ducking for cover before we realized who was firing. Those damned artillerymen about laughed their asses off. They wouldn't have thought it was so funny if we had turned our turrets around and blasted them. We wouldn't have done that, but I am sure it was in everybody's mind. We felt pretty sheepish. Most of us hadn't realized just how jumpy we were getting. When you have to be in the field all the time, reactions like that will sometimes save your life. You get to where any loud or unexpected noise will send you scrambling for cover. We had been going out on operations for a pretty long stretch without seeing much action, and Tet was just around the corner. We knew when the Tet offensive started we would have more than enough action to keep us busy.

Chapter 9

WE TOOK TO THE FIELD AGAIN on another sweeping operation. Our routine usually didn't vary that much from week to week. The infantry working with us was walking ahead of the tanks in an effort to search out any antitank mines. We were making moderate progress when one of the men on the ground stepped on a tripwire connected to a grenade. Two men went down instantly. It is a very shocking thing to see two healthy young men walking along one minute, and the next minute see them writhing and convulsing on the ground with their bodies spouting blood. It's a sight you never forget.

I couldn't say enough about the brave and compassionate medics in Vietnam. Their courage and devotion to duty was an inspiration to every soldier who ever served in Vietnam and watched them in action. We always had at least one medic along with our outfit when we were in the field. Sam Davis was with us today, and he never once hesitated. He ran right out in that booby trapped area and started caring for the wounded men. I have watched our medics run out in the middle of mine fields, booby traps, and gunfire to give aid, with never a thought to their own safety. They always put their comrades first and foremost in every instance I ever knew.

One of the two guys on the ground received fairly light wounds, and the other man was in bad shape with chest, leg, and head wounds. Sam stopped the bleeding and had the man stabilized before the "dust-off" came on the scene to take the men to the hospital. After calling in the dust-off we continued on our sweep.

Whenever we approached a hedgerow during our operations, the lead tank would fire a canister round from the main gun through it before we tried to drive the tank through. A canister round contained hundreds of steel pellets. It made the main gun just like a giant shotgun. We used the canister round to trip any booby traps that might have been set in the hedgerow. The cannister round was also very effective for fending off a close range attack or for clearing away jungle underbrush.

There were many areas where we could see large bomb craters where B-52s had pounded enemy positions in previous battles. While my tank was moving through one of these areas, a man walking behind our tank shouted at me and pointed to a spot directly behind us. I looked back and I realized he was pointing at a one-thousand-pound bomb that had failed to detonate. The track of the tank had caught on the tail fin of the bomb and partially unearthed it. I thought to myself, *Ohhhh, shit!* My hair really stood on end. I was afraid to even breathe until we had put a bunch of distance between us and that dud bomb. I had seen a picture once of a tank that had been hit by a bomb that size and there wasn't much left of it.

We set up a night perimeter and put up our RPG fence and trip flares. According to Intelligence, the Vietcong activity in this area was supposed to be on the increase, so we were extra careful. I put claymore mines in front of our position, and beneath the claymores I placed a trip flare with the pin pulled. We had all heard stories of how the VC would slip up and turn the claymores around so that they pointed in our direction. When set off, they would blow us away instead of the enemy. I was hoping the trip flares would give anyone messing around with my claymores a big surprise.

We sent a team out to our front as a listening post, or L.P., to give us advance warning of any enemy soldiers approaching our position. We were set for the night now and all we could do was wait. At three in the morning the men in the L.P. started firing. In a few seconds they came running back to our position on the double. They had heard a group of Vietcong approaching and had opened fire on them. The surprised Vietcong ran like hell. Five minutes later we heard a mortar start firing. Everyone ducked for cover as the mortar shells hit all around our position. Our forward observer called in a fire mission to the artillery and we soon heard the big shells screaming overhead. They rained down all around our position and on the suspected mortar position. We received some light rifle fire, but after the artillery barrage all we heard was silence, save for the ever present "fuck you" lizards yelling their obscenities in the distance.

With the coming of dawn we started to pack up and get ready for another day. Junior went out to take in the claymore mines and forgot all about the trip flares that were planted beneath them. He picked up a claymore and with a loud pop, the trip flare went off. Junior was so startled he dropped the mine and ran quickly back toward the tank. When he dropped the claymore it landed directly on top of the trip flare and the intense heat set the claymore off. We heard a loud explosion and everyone hit the dirt. We thought we were receiving incoming fire again. When Junior told us what he had done we put two and two together and figured out what happened. We had a good laugh on ourselves after we realized no one was hurt.

A reconnaissance team was sent out to check the surrounding area for signs of our attackers. They found three Vietcong bodies and signs that other bodies were dragged away. The Vietcong always tried to hide any casualties they sustained so that we could never get an accurate count of how many men we had killed. The recon team determined that the enemy had vacated the area, so we proceeded on our way.

Domingo was always giving Junior a hard time while he was driving. He was never content just to let Junior do his job; he had to always be telling him to "turn left," "turn right," "watch out for that barbed wire," and so on. After listening to his bullshit awhile Junior would unhook his microphone and tell Domingo that it was on the blink. One day Domingo told Butters and me, "I just can't understand why that guy has so much trouble with his headset. I've had the communications shop check it out and they can never find anything wrong." I don't think he ever did figure out that Junior just got tired of hearing his shit and tuned him out. Bill and I never did clue him in. We were enjoying ourselves too much. It did our hearts good to see Domingo so frustrated. He could be a real pain in the ass at times, so we found it hard to muster the least bit of compassion toward him.

Off in the distance we could see air force planes making bomb runs on a patch of jungle. They were dropping napalm, and it was a beautiful, fascinating sight off in the distance. We could not understand how anyone could survive such an attack. Year after year the Vietnamese did survive, and they kept on resisting.

We had great respect for the Vietnamese fighting man, but in our hearts, we knew we were better. Every one of us felt that we were forced to fight with one hand tied behind our backs. The North Vietnamese Army came south to fight, but we were not allowed to pursue him into his sanctuaries across the borders to the north. Most of the time we had to call in for permission before we could even shoot at him. We would take thousands of casualties from booby traps before the war ended, but we weren't allowed to set booby traps. The American soldier took a piece of ground only to pull out and give it back to the enemy a few days later. In most cases, after a week or a month went by, we would have to take the same ground all over again. This happened time after time all over Vietnam. This was not World War I or II, where you gained ground and kept it. We never heard of front lines, except as an abstract expression. The battle lines were wherever Charlie decided to hit, and that could be any place in Vietnam, at any given time. The people of Vietnam hated us, and we soon learned to hate them. We weren't fighting for flag and country so much as we were just trying to survive our tour of duty and get the hell out of Vietnam.

Chapter 10

WE FINALLY MADE IT BACK TO BASE CAMP, where everyone was able to relax. Butters, Underwood, and I cleaned weapons and greased the tank road wheels by day. When night time rolled around, we hit the various NCO and EM clubs on base. We consumed as much beer and whiskey as our systems would allow. Boozing it up was really the only form of recreation open to us, and we took advantage of it. During this stand-down of two days we put the tank back into fighting trim, got drunk, and were ready to go out again.

We headed out the west gate of Cu Chi early in the day. Our mission was to patrol the area of the Ho Bo Woods and slow down infiltration in the area. It so happened that the Ho Chi Minh trail branched out into this area as a main supply route to the Vietcong operating in and around Saigon. Whenever we had to make sweeps in this region everyone was really on their toes. The Ho Bos were most definitely Indian country, meaning that Charlie moved around pretty freely. This was his turf.

We had a Kit Carson scout with us on this trip. A Kit Carson scout was a former Vietcong who had surrendered under the Chieu Hoi program, which means "open arms" in Vietnamese. Some of these guys were real handy to have around, and others were worthless. We did not really trust anyone too much who we knew might have killed some of our people in the recent past. Our Chieu Hoi's name was Lee and he was one of the better scouts to come our way.

As we were driving along on our sweeping operation, a soldier of the First of the Fifth Mechanized Infantry threw a grenade in one of the tunnels in our path. As we pulled away the grenade exploded and started a small chain reaction of other explosions. We stopped to investigate this tunnel complex a little closer. Any time we got a secondary explosion we could bet on finding an enemy ammo cache. Our executive officer, Lieutenant Green, ordered us to set up a protective perimeter around the tunnel complex so we could provide security to the men who would investigate the tunnels.

As we sat there waiting, Butters and I decided to look around a little bit ourselves. This whole area had been bombed by B-52s at one time, so many of the caves and tunnels had been collapsed by the big bombs. Our men were soon finding ammo by the ton. I saw a box sticking half out of a bomb crater. Bill and I were just a little bit leery of yanking on it for fear of tripping a booby trap. Lee, our Kit Carson scout, came along and he motioned for Bill and myself to stand back. He bent over and soon had a box of 57mm recoilless rifle shells wrestled loose from the remnants of a tunnel. Lee had shown us there was no danger of trip wires, so we started digging to see what else we could find. After some laborious digging, Bill and I found a full case of Chinese made machetes which we passed out to everyone in the company for souvenirs. As we dug a little farther down, we came upon some busted cases of Chicomm grenades. We stacked these in a pile with the rest of the captured ammunition so the shit hooks could carry it away for demolition. We were now finding the potato masher style grenades with busted handles and damaged detonators. They had been damaged quite a bit by the bombing. Bill and I were getting pretty nervous about handling this potentially dangerous ammo.

This stuff in such poor condition could blow up in our faces at any time. We decided it would be smart to quit while we were ahead, so back to the tank we went.

We were taking a beer break when over the horizon comes two or three choppers circling our perimeter. When they had satisfied themselves that the area was safe and secure, they sat down. Well, as big as you please, out pops a full bird colonel, a lieutenant colonel, and a major. Trotting along right behind them was an enlisted man with his camera and notebook. They all looked around the tunnel complex asking questions of everyone. What I saw next pissed me and everybody there completely off. The brass hats strolled on over to a shallow ditch, picked up a couple shovels, and waited there smiling, while the photographer took their pictures. Those goddamned brass-hatted bastards were taking credit for all of the hard, dangerous work we had been doing for the past six hours. I just stood there with a stunned look on my face, boiling mad. I wasn't the only one to witness this bullshit. As those officers re-entered their choppers and took off I doubted if they realized how lucky they were to get away without being shot out of the sky by their own men. I know I sure wouldn't have felt the least bit of remorse had that happened. We had found one of the biggest stashes of communist munitions of the whole year. It amounted to tons of supplies that Charlie would never use against us. After the brass left, we caved in the remaining tunnels with explosives and said the hell with it. We didn't mind doing our job and risking our lives for something worthwhile, but we were damned if we were going to keep it up when a bunch of brass-hatted primadonnas were going to take all the credit. No wonder so many officers were killed in this war by their own men if this was any example of leadership.

We remounted our vehicles and continued our search for the Vietcong. The Ho Bo Woods were full of booby traps and antitank mines, so it came as no great surprise when our tank hit a large mine. The dust and smoke really flew. After waiting for the air to clear, Domingo and I surveyed the tank for damage. This time a quick repair job in the field was not going to get us by. The mine had blown off three road wheels, busted two torsion bars and mangled the track. As in most cases, we had taken no casualties. We did have to call for a VTR, which stands for "Vehicle, Tank Recovery" in army jargon. These large, powerful, tanklike vehicles were our workhorses. They were the wreckers, cranes, and tow trucks of the armored units. After hooking on to our tank they towed us on back to Cu Chi.

The mechanics soon realized that our tank's hull was warped so badly it would have to be scrapped. The 3/4 Cavalry were just starting to get the new lightweight Sheridan tanks, so we went over to their motor pool and picked up one of their old M-48s to replace our damaged tank. I was really glad we didn't have to switch over to the lightweight Sheridan tanks. I knew there was no way that lightweight little tank could take a hit by a large mine and allow the crew to live. This assumption proved to be correct. The small Sheridan just couldn't absorb the punishment of the heavier and older M-48 tanks. As I looked my replacement tank over I noticed the 3/4 Cavalry used a rope lanyard as well as the electrical switch to fire the main gun. I figured they must use the manual device for a backup, in case the electrical solenoid failed to trip the trigger.

We got the tank back to our motor pool and began to switch our belongings and weapons over. We also made a few modifications to suit our needs. We welded on a larger bustle rack to carry our gear, and an extra fifty mount for the loader. We always had to cut part of the front fenders off the new tanks, but this one already had that done to it. If the fenders were not cut back at least a foot, they would get beat back into the tracks from driving in rough terrain. It was better to just get rid of them instead of wasting time in the field trying to get them untangled from the tracks.

Lieutenant Solars gave me the surprise of my life. After my excursions around that VC tunnel complex someone decided our unit needed a tunnel rat, so they recommended me for tunnel rat school. I had to go to classes on tunnels for two or three days so I could be the company tunnel rat. To say I was less than pleased with this new development would be an understatement. After I had gone to the tunnel rat school at Cu Chi, I learned a lot of things about VC tunnels that I had not known before. I found out they used booby traps, punji stakes, and poisonous snakes to protect their secret lairs. Now, I ain't crazy about snakes, and I'm afraid that after I received all this good training I said, "No damn way; you get some other fool to be your damn tunnel rat." I just couldn't see much of a future in the business, and I had a strong desire to stay healthy.

Chapter 11

ON THE DAY OF FEBRUARY 25, 1969, we were ordered to patrol throughout the area. So far today, we hadn't seen any trace of enemy activity. Sergeant Domingo was his usual cheerful self and Junior had unhooked his commo helmet already. It wasn't even noon yet and Domingo was as grouchy as a bear. We hit some old concertina wire that started to wrap around the tracks and Sergeant Domingo told me to take some pliers and cut it loose. I was working as fast as I could and trying to keep that rusty barbed wire from cutting me to ribbons while I worked. Domingo started shouting at me to hurry it up and then he grabbed up an old piece of tree limb that was lying on the tank and threw it at me. It hit me on the back of the helmet. That was the last goddamned straw. That cocky bastard had been ragging the whole crew for quite a while now, and I was fed up. I picked up that stick and winged it back at him as hard as I could. Regretably it buzzed right by his ear, missing by scant inches. I told him, "You get off that tank and I'll whip your ass right here and now!" He said, "Now, you don't want to do that." I said, "The hell I don't. If you don't get off my back, you're going to find out quick enough." From that day on, Domingo wasn't so quick to jump down my throat. He wasn't quite as friendly, but I really didn't care. He was never that friendly from the very start, so I didn't feel as though I had lost that much. I respected his ability as a soldier, but as a human being he left a lot to be desired. I got back on the tank and nothing else was ever said about that incident.

We were just coming up to a hootch on the edge of some old dried up rice paddies when an old lady came out and started to flag us down. We stopped to see what she wanted. The old gal didn't speak any English, but she pantomimed that there was a minefield ahead. This was pretty unusual for a person this far out in the boonies to offer any assistance to the Americans and we were a mite suspicious of her motives. Just to be on the safe side, we gave her a couple of boxes of C rations as a thank you gift and the mechanized infantry dismounted a couple of men with mine detectors to walk ahead of the column to clear the trail in front of us. In no time they found a couple of mines in our path and blew them up with sticks of C-4. As they continued on, we heard the roar of an antitank mine blowing up. To our horror we watched as one of the men from the mine sweep team was lifted high into the air amidst smoke, dirt, and debris. He fell back to earth as limp as a rag doll, minus both legs and God knows what else. When the smoke and dust settled a medic ran forward to offer what assistance he could. There was not much he could do until the medivac arrived to take the man away. He was alive, but just barely, and I don't think he had a prayer for survival. I remember thinking, *Dear God, if that ever happens to me I hope somebody puts a .45 to my head and puts me out of my misery.* After the mine sweep team stopped finding mines, they got back on their tracks and we proceeded through the minefield in single file. I thought we had made it safely through when we felt a tremendous blast. Our tank had hit another mine. We carefully dismounted to see what damage had been done. Two road wheels, hub and all, had been blown off the axle. Since we were in an open area, the column went on without us, leaving a personnel carrier and four infantrymen to help provide security while we worked on the tank. Junior sat on top of the turret near one of the fifties and stood guard while Bill and I did what we could for our crippled vehicle. The sun was bearing down and we were really anxious to be out of this minefield. We were racking our brains trying to figure out a way to get that tank rolling, but we weren't having much luck. I finally hit on the idea of just setting the hub back on the axle to keep it from dragging against the track. This would ruin the axle, but at least it would get us back to base camp safely. We were still working when the column returned. When the lead tank of the column was about fifty yards away it hit another mine. Butters and I didn't realize what the explosion was at first. We dove into that old mine crater, right on top of each other. We untangled ourselves and looked to see what had happened. Junior was holding his leg where a piece of shrapnel had torn into his knee. We looked over at the personnel carrier and one of the men up top had been hit also. The shrapnel had bounced off the tank and a large chunk had gone completely through his flak jacket and into his chest. He was really in a bad way. The medic started working on him right away and I bandaged Junior up as best I could. Junior's wound didn't seem too serious at the time, but he was in a lot of pain. By the time the medivac arrived, the man with the chest wound was unconscious. We all hoped that he would make it. Butters and I loaded Junior onto the chopper and watched it fly out of sight. That was the last time I saw Junior. I later learned that he had lost his kneecap and was sent back to the United States.

Bill and I went back to work on the tank and got the road wheels back on. It was a temporary repair job at best, but we had had enough of that place. We had been sitting there a long while and there was a good chance of a mortar team zeroing in on us if we didn't get a move on.

We started back to base camp at a very slow pace. We didn't want to burn out that axle before we got home. We kept a close watch on it, and when it got cherry red we would stop for a short while until it cooled off. By the time we got back to our base camp the axle was nearly gone, but at least we had made it. It was real late in the afternoon by the time we pulled into Cu Chi.

I filled up with hot chow at the mess hall, and then I took a cold shower. Even a cold shower felt great by now. We had mail call and it sure was nice to hear from everyone back home. I received a few birthday cards which reminded me that I would be twenty years old the following day. I sat down with a cold beer and started answering my mail. I had gotten behind quite a bit in the past three days, so it took me over an hour to catch up. I think that nearly every time I wrote home I would ask Dad to send me a bottle of whiskey. I was hoping it might arrive in time for me to celebrate my birthday. I knew how slow the mail could be over there, so I really didn't expect any miracle. I drank another beer and started on over to the mess hall with Butters to get a late snack, but the door was locked and not a soul was around. I wasn't going to let that stop me, so I tore a hole in the screen door, unlocked it, and we went right on in. It was very dark and I didn't have a flashlight. We started fumbling around in the kitchen till I tripped over some pots and pans, causing a hell of a racket. The cook must have been close by because here he came, a rifle in one hand and a flashlight in the other hand. He said, "Dammit, you guys, what the hell are you doing? I was about ready to shoot you! I thought you were gooks or something." We allowed as how we just wanted to have a little midnight snack and meant no harm. We got chased out and had to make do with C rations from off the tank. I could see it now, "Toby Brant, shot down in the line of duty while filching cheese."

Chapter 12

THAT DAY WAS ONE OF THE RARE TIMES I was allowed to sleep late and I took advantage of it. Once I had decided to haul myself out of the sack I ambled on over to the mess hall to load up on some delicious powdered eggs, stale coffee, and cold toast. I had heard that there was a steam bath and massage parlor on base. I was very anxious to try it out. I got the directions from a friend and walked over. I paid the lady at the desk and she gave me some clean towels and propelled me towards the showers. They actually had hot water, a luxury beyond belief. I took a nice long shower and then settled into a warm cozy steam cabinet where I got totally relaxed. It was terribly warm after a while, but it felt great. Once they decided that I was properly cooked, I got out and took another shower. That was the first time since coming to Vietnam that I felt really clean. I decided to get the works, so I was shown to a small cubicle where I got a massage from my head to my toes. By the time I was ready to leave that place I was feeling like a new man. I silently resolved to enjoy that experience again.

I was running low on film, razor blades, and other items, so while I had some time off I went over to the PX and picked up the needed items. On the way back to the company area, I noticed a small giftshop where I picked up a couple of dolls to mail to my little sisters back home. I knew they would get a thrill out of them. The rest of the day I took it easy with some of the other men in our unit.

We sat around swapping tales and drinking beer.

I went to the supply sergeant's hootch to pick up my laundry and it was totally screwed up, as usual. Every damn time my laundry came back I got a different size uniform. I hardly ever got the same clothes back that I sent out. That can be most frustrating after a long period of time. A person never ever wanted to send any white clothes to the laundry. They always came back the color of mud. I really don't know how the laundry was done, but it must have been on a rock in the dredge ditch.

We were waiting until the mechanics were able to get to work on our tank, and we were faced with the prospects of finding a new driver to replace Junior. In the meantime we stayed in at Cu Chi and enjoyed the rest break.

Late at night, on the twenty-sixth of February, Bill and I were sitting outside the hootch talking when we started hearing a commotion near the perimeter. The automatic weapons fire was increasing in tempo. It sounded as though it was coming from the north and northeast of us. Our CO got a call and was informed that our base camp perimeter had been attacked. An estimated fifty Vietcong had penetrated our defenses and were now inside the wire. We were put on full alert. Bill and I knew our tank was not in the best condition, but we could move well enough to make it to the wire and we could still shoot all of our weapons. We requested permission to take our tank out to the perimeter and fight. The CO was not ready to make a decision yet, so Bill and I went on out to the motor pool and loaded up our weapons, then waited for orders. As we sat there on the tank we could see explosions and fire shoot high into the air in the direction of the helicopter pads. The VC were blowing up the big Chinooks. We sat there feeling frustrated and helpless, knowing we could do some good if only we could get our crippled tank into action. We were ready to go if the captain gave us the go-ahead; but there we sat, like a couple of kids on the football team who had been benched.

We heard a loud whistling sound in the sky and ducked down inside the tank. The noise could only come from one source, 122mm rockets. These were the only thing Charlie had in our area that resembled heavy artillery. Those rockets could be pretty devastating. After we heard them explode we poked our heads out to see what damage had been done. A group of men were converging on the mess hall. Our cook, a real likable young guy from New York, had been out feeding some dogs in front of the mess hall when the rocket hit. It went through the roof and out the front wall of the building, exploding on the ground in front of the mess hall. Our cook was killed instantly along with two of his pets. You didn't have to be out in the boondocks in Vietnam to get killed. Anyone at any time or any place could buy the farm in this country. Another rocket exploded in the company area next door to us. It went through the roof of a hootch, going off between two sleeping men. Miraculously, neither one of the men were injured. Things happended that way sometimes.

I was still trying to get permission to go gook hunting, but the captain was afraid the Vietcong would try to blow up the tanks in our motor pool. He had us pull our tank near the headquarters building and stand guard for the rest of the night or until we got the all clear. We were about three-fourths pissed off, but we did as we were told. Lieutenant Solars told us to fire a burst from our fifty over the heads of anyone we saw moving, and if they did not identify themselves, blow them away. A short while later, I saw a figure walking near the motor pool fence, so I fired a short burst way in the air over his head. I was pretty sure he was one of our sentries but I was feeling kind of ornery and bored, so I fired anyway. You wouldn't believe all the excitement that caused. An officer started to chew me out, and I just told him, "Hey, I was just following orders. I saw someone move out there, so I fired over his head. If you don't like it, talk to the lieutenant, but get off my ass." They soon left after modifying my orders. Bill smiled at me and said, "Toby, you crazy bastard." He really got a kick out of that dumb stunt. We sat there all night long and never saw one VC. That morning I heard there was a hell of a man hunt going on. There were still several Vietcong being shot or rounded up. As long as there was still a chance of some of them hiding on base at Cu Chi none of us were going to sleep too heavy.

Lieutenant Green got hit by a small piece of shell fragment from the exploding 122s. It hit him in the back and it was no bigger than a speck. It looked as if someone might have pricked him with a lead pencil. He put himself in for a Purple Heart and everyone in the company teased him unmercifully for several days afterwards. He was a good man, though, and a good officer, so we didn't really get down on him. We just enjoyed giving him a hard time. He had as much right to get his ticket punched as the rest of the officers over there, and more than most.

That day was my twentieth birthday, and I got to celebrate it by working on the tank all day long. The mechanics had finally gotten around to repairing our tank, but we had to be there to assist them whenever necessary. Everything on a tank is heavy, so when it comes to making repairs you have to be ready to do a lot of lifting and straining.

Later in the day our CO held a memorial service for our departed comrade. Taps were played at the end of the service, and there is no more mournful or sadder tune in the world. There were not too many of us that didn't have lumps in our throats, and dry eyes were few. Even to this day when I hear taps I have a hard time not choking up.

We got our old and battered second-hand tank going again and awaited our assignment for the coming day. It looked like the '69 Tet Offensive was under way.

Chapter 13

BILL BUTTERS AND I were not too overjoyed with our replacement tank because it was nearly worn out when we received it. A tank's life span is pretty short under combat conditions. It receives a lot of hard use under very adverse conditions. With a lot of hard work from all of the members of our crew, plus the added help of our motor pool mechanics, we got her shaped up and ready to roll.

Sergeant Domingo was leaving for R and R that day, so I was placed in command of the tank during his absence. I was just a little nervous about being responsible for three men's lives. Knowing this, I was determind to do the best I possibly could and hopefully make all the right decisions.

Three tanks out of the First Platoon were ordered to proceed to Trang Bang, a small village near the Cambodian border. Trang Bang was a known trouble spot, so it always paid to be on your toes in its vicinity. We had been ordered to set up an outpost along the particularly troublesome stretch of road where the Vietcong were always planting mines and causing trouble. A large convoy of supply trucks that were destined for a small fire support base directly to the north of us was running late. We had been ordered to keep the road open until they arrived, and then escort them on in to the fire support base.

We had a long wait before the convoy was even expected, so we tried to get as comfortable as possible. Bill and I had an old canopy from a large parachute flare, so we rigged up a small tent to shade us from the sun. We broke out a couple of folding cots and got settled in. As we waited, one of us stood watch at all times. The danger at this time of the day was minimal, but I was taking no chances. I was more than a little surprised when one of our hootch girls from base camp came riding up on a Honda that had saddle bags full of beer thrown over the back. I was concerned about how she knew our location. If she was so well informed of our movements, then how much did the Vietcong know? It was something to ponder and worry about. This hootch girl and a companion were peddling beer. Our beer supplies were getting very low, a terrible situation to befall a tanker, so we purchased a six pack at an exorbitant price. We caught up on our letter writing, listened to Ray Stevens sing "Guitarzan" on the radio, and drank beer for most of the day.

The sun was starting to get low in the sky and we were getting worried; that convoy still had not shown up and it would soon be dark. Our tank was separated from the other two tanks by at least a quarter of a mile. If we were attacked we would have no one there to protect our flanks. The sun had now set and it would be pitch dark in a matter of minutes. Our situation had gone from one of comfort to very tense. Finally, just after dark, the convoy rolled into sight. The first tank took up a position at the head of the convoy, the second tank pushed into the middle, and our tank, the last to pull out, was to provide a rear guard. Just as the last vehicle of the convoy was ready to pass, we began to back around and take up our position to the rear. As soon as we started out a Vietcong recoilless rifle team opened fire on our tank. I caught sight of the flash out of the corner of my eye. In a split second an explosion rocked the tank. Butter's helmet was blown off and a box of .50 caliber ammunition that had been sitting on the front fender of the tank popped open as it was blown into the air, and a belt of .50 caliber ammo wrapped itself around the driver's neck. I knew our tank had taken a hit, but I had no idea of how bad it was or how much damage we had sustained. The first thing I did was to aim the main gun toward our attackers. I pulled the trigger and was greeted by a faint click and silence. A sick feeling arose from the pit of my stomach and I yelled to the driver, "Get this son of a bitch out of here!" We were backing up so as to have our heavy frontal armor facing the enemy. Butters and I were both firing our fifties furiously. I had learned a long time ago that the best defense is a strong offense. Even if you do not hit anything there is a good chance your return fire will at least spoil your attacker's aim. I kept telling Butters to keep his damn head down. I felt he was sticking his neck out a little too much, and he was too close a friend to lose because of carelessness. As we gained the road, I told the driver, "Turn around now and let's move on out." We had to turn gently because our track had been hit and I had no idea what shape it was in. All I knew was that if the track broke we were sitting ducks out there with a main gun that was useless. Just as we got turned around another explosion sprayed the tank with dirt and shrapnel. That last shot had been a near miss. We were now moving and were soon out of range. Bill and I kept up sporadic firing on either side of the road for quite a distance just in case another ambush was in the making. We were determined to keep them off balance. After driving for about a mile we came into a small village outside the fire support base and we ceased firing. I had reported our predicament over the radio, but as busy as I had been, and somewhat rattled to be sure, my report was not as clear as it could have been. I then settled down and gave a more precise report to headquarters. Our left track was making a thumping noise, so I was really relieved when we reached the safety of the base camp.

After parking the tank, Bill and I carefully checked the tank for damage. The left-front steel road wheels had been mashed flat. Out track had been blown half in two, the left-front fender was bent into the air and our searchlight had been knocked out. We had been exceedingly lucky that the track had held together long enough to get us to safety. We were also very lucky indeed in the fact that not one of us had been hit or even scratched by the flying shell fragments.

That night we were still pretty excited by our narrow escape, so we partied down and got as drunk as lords while we congratulated one another on our good fortune. The next day we ordered parts from Cu Chi and got down to the business of making repairs. I was really worried about that main gun misfiring. I carefully checked it over and soon realized that the solenoid that trips the trigger was unhooked. To my horror, and embarrassment, it dawned on me why the 3/4 Calvalry had that damned rope lanyard hooked up. I felt pretty foolish that I hadn't checked that out a little closer. It just hadn't occurred to me that they would unhook the electrical firing device and use a stupid clothesline rope as the primary firing system. It took me less than five minutes to make a minor adjustment and put the cannon in order again. Once all the work had been finished we were able to take it easy for awhile.

We partied down again that night. There is nothing more exhilarating than facing the enemy and living to brag about it. We were really lucky and we knew it. If the VC had shot two inches higher we would have blown our track completely in two. He then could have polished us off at his leisure because it would have taken quite a while for the other two tanks to get untangled from the convoy and back to our position. By that time it would have been too late for me or my crew.

We were feeling pretty cocky by now, and it was just as well, for we were headed back into the bush tomorrow where, in all likelihood, our cockiness would turn back into fear and caution.

Chapter 14

THIS WAR WAS NO LONGER AN ADVENTURE to me. I could now see war for what it really is, nothing but sweat, dust, filth, cruelty, fear and death. This was not a Hollywood portrayal of war, this was the real thing, and for me the novelty had worn off. Speaking of novelty, our company commander had a fifty-caliber machine gun mounted on his jeep. I presumed he had visions of "Rat Patrol" on his mind. I saw them fire that thing one time. They dropped the windshield down on the jeep and fired it forward as the jeep stood still. That little jeep started hopping up and down like a rubber ball. It kept scooting backwards for as long as they were firing. The CO was afraid to fire that big fifty sideways for fear it would turn his jeep over. After seeing that, I figured so much for "Rat Patrol" and TV heros.

For the most part, we occupied the next three or four days on endless patrols through dusty, dried-up rice paddies, down barren dirt roads and fighting brush, heat, and insects. Each day would culminate in making the endless repair on vehicles pushed beyond their limits.

We all drank beer in my outfit, and we enjoyed it in base camp or in the field, but I never once saw a man drink too much, or even approach drunkenness when we were in the field. It was a pleasant way to replace lost moisture as much as anything.

The old tank we had gotten from the 3/4 Cavalry had all but given out by this time. I must confess I was happy to see that old hunk of junk go by the wayside. It was getting to the point where we were always broken down, and the old girl was just too unreliable. I was ordered to go to Long Binh, just outside of Saigon, to pick up a new tank. The platoon leader of the second platoon's name was Sergeant Rasberry. I was to accompany him and Bob Barbre, his tank driver, to the supply depot as they needed a tank also. Sergeant Rasberry's platoon called themselves Rasberry's Raiders, a hard name to forget. Bob Barbre was a good-natured boy with a lot of guts who hailed from a small town in Southern Illinois called Carmi. Since I was from the central part of the state we struck up a conversation and got to be good friends. Bob was later wounded by an RPG and was blinded in both eyes. He also had to have a steel plate implanted in his skull. I saw Bob a few times after I got back to the States. He died of a heart attack only a couple of years after he got home. Bob was only about twenty-two or twenty-three years old, and there is no doubt in my mind that his early death was a result of his wounds.

We rode down to Long Binh in the back of a two-and-a-half-ton truck. It was only about thirty or thirty-five miles, so the trip itself didn't take too long. Once we got there we naturally ran into the normal red tape. At the depot we sat around and waited for several hours for them to give us our tanks. After waiting for all this time, the supply officer showed us a couple of M-48A2 tanks. These tanks were about the same as the M-48A3s we were using except they had gasoline engines. We told him, "No way are we going to take a gasoline-powered tank. If those things get hit by an RPG, they go off like a bomb." We wanted diesels and nothing else. A diesel tank might catch fire when an RPG hit the fuel tanks, but it was much less likely to explode. The officer in charge tried his best to talk us into the other tanks because he already had them serviced and ready to go. When he realized that neither Rasberry nor myself would change our minds he told us that we would have to wait until the next day before he could have our new tanks ready to roll. It was getting close to sundown anyhow and we were not about to drive back to Cu Chi in the dark with no crew or ammo. We were more than happy to wait till in the morning to leave.

We were shown to a barracks with some empty bunks to spend the night in. As I walked around the area I noticed a bulletin board. I started reading it out of curiosity and noticed that they had a man listed as the Bronze Star winner of the month. He was a company clerk. The rear echelon motherfucker was probably one hell of a typist. I had seen everything now. I figured things must be pretty bad when the army started handing out Bronze Stars to people for keeping their nose clean for the month.

We picked up our tanks the next day and started back to Cu Chi. Our trip back went smoothly as Rasberry, Bob, and I made it without mishap. Right off the bat Sergeant Domingo started to raise hell about me being gone overnight, as if I had a choice. I told him if I had known he wanted one of those rolling bombs with a gasoline engine I would have gladly come back early. Even Sergeant Domingo wasn't that stupid.

For the rest of that day the guys in our platoon got stuck building bunkers in a new fire support base just east of Cu Chi. We labored hard filling endless rows of sandbags. We were about half afraid we might have to man those bunkers ourselves one day, so we built them as strong as we could. As each team of men finished their assigned bunkers we were allowed to go back to base camp and clean up. Cold showers, as usual!

After relaxing on my cot for a while, I heard the company clerk yell, "Mail call!" That always got a response from everyone. We all ran over to see if we had lucked out with a letter from home. Now I had been writing for a good long while to my folks requesting a bottle of good whiskey, so when I saw a great big care package for me my eyes fairly danced in anticipation. I took the package to my hootch and started to tear into it. The first thing I saw as the cardboard came ripping apart was a beautiful brand-new, beer cooler. Dad, bless his heart, was really on the ball. My mouth almost watered as I opened the lid. Inside were two large display packs of Planter's peanuts and cashews. I dug a little further and found a new transistor radio and a large chunk of styrofoam. As I grabbed up the styrofoam and ripped the tape away, I crossed my fingers. Sure enough, in a hollowed out niche was a bottle of 100-proof, grade A, bonded in the USA, Schenley's sippin' whiskey. The first thing I did was to yell for my buddy, Bill Butters. "Hey, Bill, come here, we are going to party tonight!" I didn't have to twist his arm. I said, "I never heard of this particular brand of whiskey before, is it any good?" Bill said, "You're damned right it is, Toby!" Well, we just popped the cap off and had at it. We scrounged up some beer, sat down, and started drinking that whiskey as we chased it with beer. We wanted to savor it for as long as we could, so after the first swallow or two we didn't drink too fast. We just relaxed and took it as easy as possible. Along about midnight neither one of us were feeling any pain. As a matter of fact, we had a hell of a load on, so Bill and I just turned in.

Along about three in the morning I was awakened by yells of "Incoming!" I was so drunk I could hardly see straight, but I managed to stumble out the door toward the bunker. As I fell down the bunker stairs I remember someone saying something about a rocket attack. The last thing I remembered that night was crawling onto a two-by-twelve board lying on the floor and falling asleep. I was too drunk to even walk, but I had made it to the bunker.

The next morning when I woke I was still lying on the floor of the bunker, but no one was there except me. My head was throbbing like a bass drum and I had no idea how long I had been passed out down there. I thought to myself, *Oh, shit, I hope my outfit didn't have to pull out while I've been down here wiped out.* I got to my feet and very gingerly climbed the stairs. I got to the top and blinked several times as my eyes tried to adjust to the bright sunlight streaming down. All I could do was moan. I looked into the hootch, but there wasn't anybody there. I walked carefully to the motor pool where, with a sigh of relief, I spotted Bill strapping my new beer cooler onto the tank. He allowed as how I should sit down down and get out of the sun for a while. I sure wasn't going to argue the point. If I had looked half as bad as I felt then I knew it must be serious. After drinking a couple gallons of water I helped Bill load the tank with ammunition and get everything ready to go on our new vehicle. By nightfall I was never so happy to see a bunk in my life. It had been worth it though, and I had enjoyed the hell out of my first care package from home.

Chapter 15

ON OCCASION THE THIRTY-FOURTH ARMORED had to work with the South Vietnamese Army. We usually dreaded this experience. My first patrol with the ARVNs ("Arvins") pretty well soured me for life. We started on a sweep just north of Cu Chi with the ARVNs riding along on our tanks and personnel carriers. The patrol seemed to be going routinely enough, except for the small problem of a communication gap. My Vietnamese left a lot to be desired. When we came to the rougher areas where the infantry would usually dismount and scout ahead of the tanks our trouble began. We practically had to force the Vietnamese off our vehicles at gunpoint. Those worthless bastards were afraid to leave the security of the tanks. After much threatening by their officers, and us, they finally started to dismount, but instead of fanning out the whole damn company grouped up and proceeded to walk forwark in single file. It is very difficult to search an area when no one is willing to look anywhere, except in a straight line. The Mechanized Infantry of the U.S. First Batallion, Fifth Infantry, Twenty-Fifth Division had to do all of the tricky stuff because our allies didn't have the guts to even get over twenty yards away from our vehicles. We began to see that the situation was hopeless and we said the hell with them. As we approached the Saigon River a couple of snipers opened fire. The goddamned ARVNs hit the dirt and not a one of them so much as fired a shot. Our guys opened fire and the snipers made their getaway. The ARVNs didn't make a move till after the shooting had stopped. Our officers had had about enough of this crap. We just couldn't see any point in continuing this farce. Once we had gotten rid of the Vietnamese soldiers we started to take inventory. Not only were the ARVNs pathetic cowards, they were thieving sons of bitches. We tried to watch them every minute they were on our tank, but they still managed to steal half of our poncho liners and the better part of our C rations. I cringed every time I learned that we had to work with the ARVNs.

Not every experience was quite that negative, but very few joint operations turned out to be productive. The only instance where I can recall that anything went right was a patrol northwest of Cu Chi when the ARVNs with us spotted a man and woman running away through the scrub brush. We had somehow managed to surprise them before they could get back to their hiding places. About ten ARVNs jumped off the tanks, ran them down, and killed both of them. They captured an AK-47 assault rifle, two pairs of sandals, and a large black rat that was penned up in a bamboo cage. I couldn't understand why they would want a rat until I saw one of the ARVNs make a sign like he was going to eat the evil-looking thing. My stomach flip-flopped and I nearly gagged at the thought of fricasseed rat. I vowed to never bitch about C rations again. I did think in this instance that the ARVNs showed some courage, but also a good deal of stupidity. When they started to run that couple down they literally took off like a bunch of kids chasing a kite. They displayed no discipline at all. If an ambush had been set up the ARVNs would have paid dearly.

The ARVNs' rations normally consisted of plain rice with no seasoning while they were in the field. They carried it in a cellophane bag which they would pour water into about twenty or thirty minutes before meal time. One time when we had only two Vietnamese with us on our tank we cordoned off a small village while the Vietnamese police searched it. We decided to break for lunch while we waited. I noticed the Vietnamese soldiers only had plain rice to eat and I felt kind of sorry for them. Now that I think about it, we only had plain C rations, so they may have felt sorry for us. At any rate I grabbed an old cooking pot and put their rice into it. I then added about three cans of assorted goodies from our own rations and sprinkled liberal dashes of salt, pepper, and tabasco sauce. It wasn't exactly a mulligan stew, but it didn't taste too bad. Those ARVNs acted like I had put on a real feast. Those boys dug in like they thought they had died and gone to heaven. It wasn't the same as rat stew, but it must have been okay.

The Vietnamese National Police were some real bad asses. Those guys did not mess around when it came to interrogating civilians. They would kick the hell out of anybody that didn't give them the right answers. I didn't know how good they were at fighting armed VC but they sure were bad when it came to beating up defenseless kids, women, and old men.

The South Vietnamese Army had a high desertion rate due to the fact that their officers often cheated them out of their pay and other commodities. The officers would skim supplies and sell them on the black market. The enlisted men in turn would often sell equipment to the VC or on the black market to make up for skimpy pay and poor rations, so it was a never ending circle of corruption. After I got back to the States and I learned about the Vietnamization program I knew that the war was as good as lost. The South Vietnamese did not have the desire or fortitude to win the war against the North on their own.

Once, when I first got to Vietnam, I was driving a

tank down a country road that had concertina wire on both sides, leaving just barely enough room for the tank to get through. As I approached this narrow corridor a Vietnamese on a bicycle started to go through at the same time. I thought, *Now, would you look at that crazy guy*. I know he had to see me coming, yet on he came, peddling for all he was worth right at me. It doesn't take a mental giant to figure that it's just not too smart to play chicken with a tank when you are on a bicycle, but on he came. I was going full bore and had no place to go but straight ahead, so on I went. I fully intended to make a big greasy spot in the road out of that dumb bastard. Just as I tensed up for the collision he drove his bike into the barbed wire at the side of the road. I let out a sigh of relief as we passed by. I could see him all hung up in about three rows of concertina wire, raising hell. He could have waited until I had passed by before he came on, but for some odd reason he decided to challenge me and try to make me back down. That's about as smart as going bear hunting with a switch.

Whenever we set up an outpost by a village for any length of time we would dig a hole in the ground to bury our trash. Mostly there were empty C ration cans in it. When we pulled out the Vietnamese would dig everything up and rummage through it. One day one of the guys got the bright idea of burying a CS gas cannister with the trash. The pin was pulled so that when it was disturbed tear gas would spew all over. As we left that day we drove a little slower than normal so we could observe the results of our handiwork. Just as we expected, a bevy of civilians made a dash for the refuse pile and started to dig. The next thing we saw was people scattering in all directions, rubbing their eyes and noses. The plan was a complete success. We laughed so hard our sides ached. Thereafter we made the CS gas-in-the-dump trick standard operational proceedure.

Sometimes when we went on thunder runs at night we would pass through small villages. We always carried hand-held star cluster signal flares on our vehicles. They were real handy for firing at straw roofs. We were supposed to fire them and parachute flares into the air for illumination, but it was just too tempting. Most of us aimed them at the roofs to see if we could set them on fire. I don't think we ever hit anything, but it wasn't because no one tried. It is no wonder the Vietnamese didn't like us, but I guarantee they got their licks in, too.

I never had much of an opportunity to get to know the Vietnamese; maybe my attitude toward them would have been a little different. The only Vietnamese I was around for any length of time were our hootch girls back at base camp. One of them was killed the morning our base camp was attacked during Tet. She was spotted trying to penetrate the perimeter and she was shot. It made us all think twice before we talked about an upcoming mission or said anything that the enemy might use against us. We didn't trust any of the civilian helpers. There was no way of knowing whose side they were on.

Chapter 16

MARCH 2, 1969, OUR PLATOON WENT ON A SWEEP into the Ho Bo Woods. We could see numerous signs of battles fought in past days, including hundreds of bomb craters and a knocked out tank forlornly rusting away in the tropical undergrowth. We had to be very careful to keep from burying our tank in the weed-choked bomb craters. A couple of times we had inadvertently driven into one of these large holes and we had to be towed out backwards by another tank. The brush was really thick in places. We weren't the only ones having trouble. The other personnel carriers and tanks were having problems with getting hung up on old tree stumps and bomb craters also. This was really rough going and we were hard-pressed to make any headway.

We had a new replacement on our tank this day. I tried to be halfway friendly to him and give him advice as we went along. I knew how it felt to be an F.N.G. (fucking new guy) and I was willing to give him the benefit of the doubt.

Our tank hit a booby trap in due course, but it must have been an antipersonnel mine judging from the size of the explosion. Domingo told me to have a look at the track to see if any damage had been done. I leaned far out over the fender to have a look. I didn't want to jump down onto the ground because of the possibilitity of stepping on other booby traps that might be scattered throughout the area. That wasn't good enough for Sergeant Domingo.

He insisted that I get completely off the tank and check for damage even though he knew the area was booby-trapped. He even had the gall to insinuate that I was a coward. I was beginning to think the dirty son of a bitch was out to get me. I got about half-mad and cautiously stepped off the tank for a better look. There was no damage sustained at all and I told Domingo so. I climbed back on the tank, doing a slow burn as I thought about the sergeant. The tank to our left-front hit another antipersonnel mine, but they didn't even bother to stop. We were lucky: We never encountered any hostile fire nor did we see any enemy troops all that day.

With the sun getting lower and lower on the cloudless horizon, we began looking for a clear area to set up a perimeter for the night. Bill Butters and I set out the trip flares, RPG screen, concertina wire and claymores. Once everything had been secured we were able to take things easy and catch up on our letter writing before it got too dark to see.

As night fell I watched the parachute flares off in the distance and I listened to the sporadic fire of artillery. I could see a far off reconnaissance plane emitting flashes of light as it took photos of the terrain below. As I observed this flashing phenomenon I noticed a long stream of tracers trying to close in on the unheeding picture taker. He was flying too high and far too fast for the VC machine gunner to even come close to his quarry. The war was going on all around us, but somehow we seemed removed from it all. Our sector was quiet and peaceful for the present, so we posted our guards and hit the sack.

Sometime in the middle of the night I was awakened by Bill shaking my boot. One of the men on guard duty had seen some movement through his starlight scope. Our whole perimeter was put on alert. We quietly watched and waited to see whether or not it was a false alarm.

Within a minute or two the VC were spotted again. Our F.O. (forward observer) calculated the coordinates on his map and called in a fire mission to the artillery. We could see the flashes of exploding shells in the vicinity where the Vietcong had been spotted. We then heard the rustling *swish* of our artillery fly over our position and heard the exploding projectiles. When the movie industry simulates artillery fire they always simulate the sound of the shells going through the air and then they show the flash of exploding shells later. This is inaccurate. In actuality, the shells are traveling faster than the speed of sound, so you always see the flash first and then you hear the sound of the shells going overhead. I suppose that old saying, "You never hear the one that gets you," springs from that.

After the initial fire mission the night reverted back to quiet and calm, with the exception of distant and remote sounds of battle far from our position. No more movement was spotted, so we settled back in for the night.

The next morning we packed everything away on our vehicles and proceeded to the area where the VC activity had been spotted during the night. As we got close we spotted two or three bodies. It was soon apparent what the VC had been doing; they had been planting antitank mines when we called the artillery in on them. Judging from one large hole in the ground, one of them had gotten nervous when the artillery hit and set off his own mine. This bit of information really pleased us. We were overjoyed at the notion that a VC had killed himself on an antitank mine meant for us. When our tank drove by the body we could see where the man had blown away the upper two-thirds of his head. All that was left of his head was the lower teeth and jaw. The new man in our tank was looking real green around the gills. It was his first body. I leaned over for a better look and said, "You're looking good, you son of a bitch!" The new man just looked at me as though I had gone off the deep end. I couldn't explain it to him, but in another month he would get great pleasure from such a sight also. He would just have to learn in his own way, if he lived long enough.

We were all in high spirits and it was time for us to go back to base camp. This patrol had been one of our better ones. We hadn't been shot at one time, yet we got a body count, and our tank had sustained no damage. All we had to do was clean the dust from our weapons and grease the tank road wheels.

Our medic rode back in with us, and he was a real character. We always liked to have Sam along on any patrol. It gave us one more man to help us pull guard duty and we felt a lot more secure knowing we had someone who could take care of us in an emergency. Sam, unlike some of the medics, always liked to carry a weapon. Once, when we were at a small fire support base, Sam was assigned to our tank. We were going on patrol the next day, so I asked him if he would like to borrow a weapon from us. He said, "You're damned right; what have you got?"

"Well," I said, "I've got an M-60 machine gun. Do you know how to fire it?" He said, "Damn right; how do you load the son of a bitch?" I showed him how to load and fire the machine gun, so he stood up on the front fender of the tank and fired it toward the jungle during a test fire period. Sam was pretty small guy, and when he opened up, the machine gun got away from him. He sprayed an arc of bullets from outside the wire and right on over the heads of some guys in a bunker next door to where our tank was parked. As the bullets flew over the heads of our next door neighbors they screamed bloody murder.

Sam finally let go of the trigger and I ran over to see if I could mollify the men who were nearly the target of Sam's unsteady aim. No one got hurt, but they were madder than hell. I didn't blame them one bit. Those boys were ready to kill on the spot. The only thing that saved Sam's bacon was the fact that he was a medic. Fortunately, all combat soldiers have the highest regard for medics, and I was able to calm them down after many apologies. From that time forward we limited Sam to an M-16 rifle. He felt real bad about the whole episode and vowed to leave the heavier guns to more experienced men.

Chapter 17

SERGEANT DOMINGO WAS GOING on another R and R one morning, leaving me in charge of the tank again. It seemed as though every time he left something heavy came up. That day was no exception. An urgent call came in to our headquarters requesting the support of our heavy tanks. My platoon was the only one available at the time, so we got the call. We weren't told right away what the situation was, but we knew it would probably be rough. No one called the heavies up without good reason. We were ordered to rush as fast as we could toward the Ho Bo Woods area. We moved with the utmost speed, and were soon on the way. The air was filled with tension and excitement as we wondered what kind of situation we would be faced with once we had reached our destination. Lt. Solars didn't keep us in the dark for long. We were told that an infantry outfit had cornered an NVA (North Vietnamese Army) regiment and they were really catching hell.

The NVA were not like the Vietcong. The VC usually used hit-and-run tactics, but the NVA were real scrappers. A hard-core NVA unit would fight right down to the last man when necessary.

As we moved closer and closer to the battle we were almost glad for a chance to close with the enemy, but we were also scared and very nervous about what lay ahead.

We hadn't had a steady driver on our tank since Junior Underwood had been hit, and we had been using whoever we could find that was available at the time. Allen Newman volunteered to drive for us today. Allen had been working in the motor pool as a mechanic. He was only two weeks away from that big freedom bird that was going to take him back to the world, but he volunteered anyway. We were really happy to have him on board. He was a steady, experienced hand that we could trust, and he had driven for us once or twice before. We also had the new man with us again today. He was riding shotgun on the back of the turret.

It didn't take long before we could hear sounds of fighting, and we could see choppers coming and going from the area just ahead. Once we reached the battle zone, Butters and I watched a Cobra gunship as he made a strafing run on the tree line to our front. As he swooped in low an NVA gunner opened up. This was the first time I had ever seen a Cobra in action. I was really amazed when he pulled the ship hard over and unleashed a barrage of rockets on the NVA gunner's position, which silenced him immediately. It was a very impressive display of maneuverability and firepower.

The NVA were nearly surrounded by the time our tanks approached the tree line. As we drew near the tree line in a line formation, my end of the formation was angled in such a manner that our tank was closer to the trees than the tank at the far end. We moved in closer and closer. Bill was down below all prepared to start shoving shells into the cannon as I fired. There were four or five soldiers to my immediate front however, and I didn't dare fire the main gun for fear of hitting our own men. The bullets were flying everywhere and I laid on my fifty, firing long bursts into the jungle. We finally started to get clear of our men to the front and I fired a high explosive round into the tree line. I then jumped back to the fifty as Bill shoved another round home. I paused for a second, trying hard to see a target, but the gooks were well concealed. As I started to fire our cannon again the bowels of our tank erupted in flame. I was blown into the air three-quarters of the way out of the hatch. As I started to fall back into the tank, I caught myself and bailed out. I hit the ground and started crawling to the rear of the tank where I noticed a soldier lying in a shallow foxhole. I looked down at my hands and saw that the skin on my hands and arms was blistered badly. I saw that Bill Butters had made it out and was making his way back toward the rear. It was then that I heard a scream come from the direction of the tank, and with horror I realized that I had left the gun tube lowered after I had fired my last shot. I knew it must be blocking Allen's escape hatch in the driver's compartment. With an icy hand around my heart I crawled back toward the tank, expecting a bullet to nail me at any time. Bullets were still buzzing like hornets and I just knew there was no way I could get back without getting hit, but with Allen still in the tank I had to try. When I got to the tank I saw Allen lying on the ground. He had somehow managed to extricate himself from that fiery hell, but his clothes were on fire and smoldering. I beat out the fire on his pants legs and shirt tail. I started to grab hold of Allen and drag him back to safety, but all of a sudden I froze up. The skin on Allen's hands, arms and face was literally peeling and flaking off. I just did not know where to grab hold of him. Suddenly he looked at me and said, "I can make it." He started to crawl forward on his elbows and I grabbed hold of his belt to assist him the best I could. We made it back to the foxhole and the medics ran forward, lifted Allen onto a stretcher, and carried him swiftly to a waiting dustoff.

It was then I became aware of the new replacement who had been riding on the back of our tank. He was the only man who had been able to get away from the tank with a weapon, and he had no injuries, yet he hadn't fired a single shot or even tried to help the rest of us. In a rage I grabbed his rifle away from him and emptied a full magazine into the tree line. He hadn't tried to cover our asses at all and I didn't much care if he had an empty weapon or not.

The engine of our tank had not been hit and it was still running smoothly. I hadn't thought much about it until it suddenly revved up, and the tank took off straight toward the tree line. I was stupefied as it went tearing into the jungle all by itself. It was uncanny, almost as if the old girl was trying to get her revenge for the mortal wounds she had received.

I now realized that I was without a weapon and my burns were hurting like hell. I ran back toward the rear, where the medivacs were busy loading up casualties. I jumped aboard a dustoff that was not yet overloaded and away we went. I started to talk to the man lying beside me on a stretcher when I realized his eyes were glazing over. With a sick feeling I realized he was dead. I nearly started to cry as I thought of his loved ones back home who were worrying and waiting patiently for his safe return. I guess my thoughts were of home and my own parents as my heart went out to the mother who would never hear the laughter of her young brave son again.

I was really depressed and I was worried about my crew's condition. I had been in command of the tank and I was responsible for my friends' lives, yet somehow I had let them down. Since then I have thought about that incident a million times, and each time I have asked myself if there was something different I could have done to change what happened. If I had stayed a little further away from the wood line until I had a clear shot, or if I had fired quicker and pumped more shells into the jungle. I still don't know the answers, and never will, but it will always haunt me.

I was really relieved when I got back to Cu Chi at the Twelfth Evacuation Hospital and I learned that everyone was alive. Allen was put into the intensive care unit and was in real bad shape. He had second- and third-degree burns over most of his body. I was sick with worry, but he wasn't allowed any visitors yet, so all I could do was pray he would be okay. Bill had burns over thirty percent of his body. He was in an awful lot of pain, but at least he was in no danger. I had burns on twenty percent of my body and was in some pain, but not as bad as the other guys. Poor Allen had to have been in agony. I hadn't been as far down inside the tank when it blew so I got burned less than the other men, with the exception of that F.N.G. that bailed off the back deck of the tank. I had a pretty low opinion of him, but after all, he was new to this shit, so I tried not to harbor too many ill feelings toward him. Right then I was just thankful to be alive.

Chapter 18

THE TWELFTH EVACUATION HOSPITAL IN CU CHI was not a large hospital complex. It was mostly a conglomeration of Quonset huts situated near Cu Chi's landing strip. The Twelfth Evac handled all types of emergencies and sickness, but it was mostly a place where the doctors and nurses tried to stabilize the worst cases brought directly in from the battlefield. They specialized in emergency procedures utilized to save the lives of men whose bodies had been torn apart in the most brutal ways. The surgeons had to contend with the problems of men who had stepped on booby traps, been hit by mortars, gunshot wounds, punji trap punctures, and severe burns from exploding vehicles, just to mention a few of the problems.

Bill Butters and I were placed in the same hospital ward and I tried to look after his needs as much as possible. I tended to hover over him like a mother hen watching her chicks. Bill and I were both in a lot of pain from our burns, but Bill was much worse off than I was. His face and arms were swollen badly, and the burned areas were constantly seeping fluids which would crust up and make it difficult for him to move his arms and hands. The day they brought us in, a nurse and an orderly removed all the loose, dead skin on our burns. They applied a white salve directly to our burns which protected our wounds from infection and helped to soothe the pain. The second day, March 5, 1969, Bill had to have help to make it to the bathroom, and I was only too glad to assist him in any way I could. I was feeling guilty about what had happened and I felt as if the weight of the world was on my shoulders. I tried to tell Bill about it, but about all I could manage to say was, "I'm sorry, Bill," and then I broke down and started to cry. I really felt bad. Bill got kind of gruff with me and he said, "Goddamnit, Toby, it wasn't your fault and I don't ever want to hear you say that again." That statement went a long way toward relieving my mind and I felt a whole lot better afterwards.

Later that day there were some more casualties brought in. I struck up a conversation with one of the guys. He had been wounded in the shoulder by an AK-47 round in the same action Bill and I had been hurt in. I described what had happened to our tank and he suddenly piped up, "You mean you guys were the ones with the runaway tank?" I admitted that it was our tank that had taken off through the tree line. He said, "When we first saw that tank take off, we thought there was someone still inside of it." I told him that the heat must have warped the accelerator linkage, causing it to rev up by itself and take off. He said, "Do you realize that your tank ran down two gooks and mashed them flatter than pancakes?"

I said, "What! Are you kidding me?"

He said, "No way, man, I saw them myself after we had managed to push the NVA back a ways."

"That is fantastic," I said. "That makes me feel a whole lot better." I told Bill about it and the guy who had given me the good news went over to Bill and repeated his story all over again. This development cheered both of us up considerably. It looked as though our old tank really did get its revenge.

A major came into the ward that afternoon and awarded everybody who had been wounded Purple Hearts. He and another officer took time to talk to each of us and listen to each man's comments, be they good or bad. Most of the guys weren't in the mood for small talk and they accepted their medals in silence.

I have never seen such a great bunch of nurses like those army nurses in Vietnam. I just can't find the words to express my admiration, love, and respect for those kind-hearted gals in white who really worked their tails off on long shifts caring for a never ending line of casualties. Still, they always took time to talk to the guys, with a kind word here and a gentle smile there, no matter how tired they were. I only wish I could remember some of their names so I could give them full credit for their unselfish acts of kindness above and beyond the call of duty.

A couple of the guys from our platoon came in to visit with Bill and me the third day we were in the hospital. The remnants of the First Platoon finally got to come in from the field and lick their wounds. Tom Dixon, a sergeant in our platoon, told us that three more tanks of the First Platoon had been knocked out before the action had finally ended the following morning. He also said that he thought our tank had been hit by two B-40 rockets, fired from an RPG launcher. I was told by other men that we had been hit by a recoilless rifle, so I was never really sure just exactly what did hit our tank. Whatever it was, it was powerful enough to penetrate our frontal armor and catch the hydraulic system on fire. In other words, they blew the hell out of things, so it doesn't really matter what hit our tank.

Bill Butters and I spent five or six days in the hospital at Cu Chi before we got the word that we were being shipped out. Bill was going to be sent to the 106th General Hospital at Yokohama, Japan, and from there he would be flown on back to the United States. It looked like the war was over for him. I was really very happy for Bill, but at the same time I felt a great loss. I knew that I would miss Bill immensely. He was the only guy I had really gotten close to the whole time I had been in-country, but he was going to be safe, so I sure wouldn't have had it any other way.

At the same time Bill got his travel orders, I received orders to go to Cam Ranh Bay to a large recuperation center where I would stay until my burns healed up. I would then be shipped back to my own outfit so I could try my luck again. I hadn't been in Vietnam very long, but I had seen all the shit I cared to see and a little bit more besides, so I can't say that I was too happy with my orders.

The last day at the Twelfth Evacuation Hospital in Cu Chi, Lieutenant Solars, our platoon leader, and Lieutenant Green, our executive officer, paid us a visit along with some of the other guys to say goodbye to us. We really appreciated their thoughtfulness. I wrote down Bill Butter's home address and we promised each other we would write and keep in touch. Bill and I did manage to exchange two or three letters while he was still in the hospital. After that we didn't hear from one another for over fifteen years. I then managed to get Bill's phone number and give him a long overdue call.

The day Bill left the hospital at Cu Chi I said, "So long," and I watched him go with a sad heart and a lump in my throat. I later learned that Allen Newman and Bill had been sent to the same hospital in Yokohama, and later to the same hospital in Texas. I was glad to hear it. Bill would be able to help look after Allen and keep me posted on how they were both doing.

I gathered up my meager belongings and prepared to board the transport plane that would take me to the hospital at Cam Ranh Bay, where I was to spend the next three weeks of my convalescence period. It was almost as hard for me to say goodbye to the nurses, doctors and Red Cross girls at the Twelfth Evacuation Hospital as it was to say goodbye to Bill. I had begun to feel very close to these wonderful people in a very short time, and it was like leaving old and trusted friends behind as I boarded the airplane and headed south.

Chapter 19

CAM RANH BAY looked like one big series of sandbars with hundreds of Quonset huts scattered around. All that sand made me feel like I had been set down in the middle of a vast desert. I was transported to the Sixth Convalescent Hospital, located right on a beautiful stretch of beach overlooking an aqua blue expanse of the South China Sea. The barracks I was assigned to was only a stone's throw away from that lovely beach.

It was nearly impossible for me to comprehend that some guys actually spent their entire tour of duty in a place like this. Can you imagine a guy getting combat pay for being a lifeguard? A lot of dudes did just that. All they had to do was swim, surf, and sunbathe. I wonder what kind of war stories they told after they got home. As for me, I thought I had died and gone to heaven.

All of the patients in the hospital were required to wear blue pajamas at all times. I guessed the locals didn't want us combat soldiers contaminating their rear echelon bootlickers.

I continued to be surprised at this place. These sons of bitches actually saluted one another, wore spit-shined boots and trousers with creases in them. I felt like I had been transported back to the United States.

I struck up a friendship with a big, dumb, friendly guy by the name of Woody Cramer. Woody had only been in the country three days when he got hit by a mortar round that sprayed his back with pieces of steel. Fortunately, none of the wounds were too serious. He did have about forty stitches scattered around here and there, holding together numerous small cuts. Woody and I were like most of the other guys here at the hospital, walking wounded and malaria cases. We checked out the hospital complex to see what was offered in the way of entertainment. There wasn't much. As we looked around we noticed the hospital complex was completely fenced off from the rest of the base. This, plus the fact that we had to wear those blue pajamas, made us feel like we were convicts or POWs rather than hospital patients. We really resented being penned up, but at least it was safe, or so we thought. It was about then that we noticed the guards walking their posts at night didn't even have loaded weapons. I told Woody, "These dumb bastards don't even know there's a war going on! If the VC attack from the sea, we are sitting ducks." About three months after I got back home I found out just how prophetic that statement really was. The Vietcong slipped into Cam Ranh Bay from the sea and had a field day. Throwing satchel charges into the hospital hootches, they hit all along the beach. There was no one to stop them, and the casualty rate was terribly high. There was absolutely no excuse for the laxness in security. It bordered on being a criminal act, considering that none of the men in the hospital complex had weapons with which to defend themselves.

Woody and I decided to go swimming, but we didn't have any swimming trunks. We did have olive drab boxer shorts with which we made do very nicely. After we had been swimming for a few minutes, a goddamn lifeguard came along and made us leave the water. It seemed they had a rule against men going swimming with bandages on. I had a gauze bandage on my left arm and Woody had a few patches of tape on his back. We went back to our hootch where we proceeded to shuck our bandages. We went swimming again and this time we were not bothered. The salt water actually softened the skin on my burns and made them feel a lot better. I believe the salt water even helped speed the healing process. Woody noticed it too because his stitches were beginning to pull. We got hold of some tweezers and scissors and I removed the stitches for Woody. He didn't want to wait around in line for a doctor, so I helped him out.

Most of our days at Cam Ranh Bay were occupied by drinking beer, swimming, sunbathing and watching outdoor movies at night. I never would have believed it at first, but I was starting to get bored with it all. There just wasn't enough to do and time really dragged.

After I had been in the hospital for a week or two, I caught a glimpse of a guy who looked terribly familiar. I saw him a couple of times after that, but I just couldn't figure out who he was. I thought he looked like a guy I had gone to school with, but I didn't really think he could be the same person. He must have noticed me staring at him because he walked over to me and asked me if my name was Toby. I knew then that he was the same person I had known from back home. I asked, "Are you Tom Pollard?" He said that he was and that he had been noticing me for a day or two also. Tom, like me, just couldn't believe he could actually be seeing someone he knew from home. I hadn't seen Tom for five years, and even then we didn't really run around together. We really hadn't been close friends back in the world, but we both were overjoyed to see someone from home. For the rest of my stay at Cam Ranh Bay, Tom and I buddied around together quite often. Tom was with the Americal Division at the northern end of Vietnam. If memory serves me right, Tom was in the hospital for a bad case of malaria. As I stated before, Tom and I hadn't been real close socially, but we had many mutual friends and old schoolmates who we talked about and traded stories about as we sipped beer in the afternoons.

It took me two weeks to get any mail from home. When I did get some, Mom was just full of questions about how I had gotten injured. I had been telling her that I was in no danger, so it was a little hard to explain to her how I had been injured. I finally had to level with her, yet I tried to spare as much detail as possible. I knew she would be a nervous wreck by now.

At the start of my third week in the hospital, it was decided that it was time for me to begin physical training. They wanted us to be in good shape when they sent us back to our units. I just about shit when I was told I would have to start running a mile every morning and every afternoon. We not only had to run, but we had to do calisthenics as well. I was in good shape, so the running and all that crap didn't really bother me physically; I just plain didn't like the idea of being forced to go through all this shit like I was some kind of dumb, green recruit.

I know this sounds stupid as hell, at least now it does, but I was getting fed up with this place and all its little tin soldiers. I was ready to go back to my own unit and get away from all these rear echelon motherfuckers and their penny ante rules and regulations. I still refused to salute officers, unless of course they were good-looking army nurses, in which case I made an exception. I would whip up a snappy regulation salute as I grinned from ear to ear. I would say, "Good morning, ma'am" with my most winning smile, but they would always give me that "Look at that horny bastard" frown in return. They always returned my salute, stuck their noses in the air, and walked right on by. Hell, even the nurses in Cam Ranh Bay were rear echelon bastards.

I wasn't really anxious to get back to the action, but I was getting sick to death of Cam Ranh Bay. Every other morning we had to be examined by a doctor to see if we were healing as we should and to weed out the guys who were well enough to be returned to their units. I got to the point where I started trying to talk the doctors into giving me a release. Nearly four weeks after I had been injured, I was given my wish. I received orders to go back to Cu Chi and the Thirty-Fourth Armored. Once I had received my orders I got to thinking about it and I could almost feel that old fear creeping back into my bones. I guess some people don't have sense enough to know when they have it made. Before I knew it, I was given a nice new issue of jungle fatigues and I was flying back to Cu Chi like the damn fool that I was.

Chapter 20

CU CHI HADN'T CHANGED MUCH since the last time I saw it, but it was different. In the four weeks I was gone I realized there were a lot of new faces and many of the old hands were missing. Some had reached the end of their tour and some were KIA or WIA. When I stepped back into the old hootch I was shocked to see that my bed had been taken and most of my personal belongings had been ripped off. There wasn't much loyalty in the outfit, it seemed. I was hurt by the callous disregard shown for my property and self. I also noticed that the esprit de corps had seemed to diminish and morale had somehow hit rock bottom. I couldn't really tell whether all this was in my own mind or if things had really hit an all-time low. I did know that I missed Bill Butters one hell of a lot. I suppose that this affected me as much as anything, coming back and knowing my old buddy would never be back. I felt a little bit lonely and even somewhat lost. I was determined not to let myself get too friendly or close to anyone again. It wasn't that I didn't want friends, I just couldn't stand the thought of losing them; it takes too much out of a man emotionally.

I was assigned to the same old platoon with Sergeant First Class Domingo in charge. I trudged on over to the motor pool to inspect our new tank. It was a decent vehicle and it was brand-new, so it hadn't had a chance to get too filthy yet. I had lost what little enthusiasm I had had for the war when I first arrived.

I met our new loader, a young kid from Guam. I was only twenty years old, but I was beginning to feel like I was ninety. Abe Cabrican was a nice guy and he always tried hard. Abe had a gentle nature and he was easy to like. I may have been a little unfair to Abe, but I held a certain part of myself in reserve. I hoped that I could stay as remote as possible. I was never surly or mean to anyone, but I was not as friendly as I would have liked to have been. Abe had a beautiful tenor voice and he would sit around for hours singing songs for us as we drank beer and thought of home. My favorite song was "The Sloop John B." For some reason it seemed to have a haunting quality of days gone by and home.

The first patrol I went on after I had been back was a real trial for me. I was so jumpy and nervous that I was ducking at every little sound. I was really scared now that I had been hit once. I felt nearly worthless because of my nerves, but I was determined to carry on. I just kept on doing my duty like a good little soldier even though I was afraid I might fall apart at any minute. I felt ashamed of my fear and I hoped that it wouldn't show. I gradually started to settle down and get myself back together again. It wasn't easy to go back on the line, but I did it, and eventually I was my old self again. It took nearly three weeks and several patrols for me to get back into the swing of things.

We had one assignment where we went outside the wire at Cu Chi to give a fire demonstration to some ARVN marines. This was the first time I had see an ARVN unit that looked like they were thoroughly professional. The South Vietnamese soldiers I had seen up to that time looked and acted as slovenly as pirates. They also had the morals of pirates when it came to pilfering anything and everything that wasn't tied down. Those marines, however, didn't steal a thing from us. They looked to be as disciplined and confident as any U.S. unit I had seen. I didn't get to see them in action, but I would have bet a month's pay that they would hold up under fire. We fired several volleys from our main guns, which seemed to impress the ARVNs immensely. We then gave them a firepower demonstration called a mad minute, where each tanker fired all of their weapons at the same time and they kept on firing until ordered to cease fire. It was a very impressive display and those ARVN marines were convinced. They were ready to become tankers on the spot. We gave the Vietnamese a complete tour of our tanks, inside and out. When we were finished, their officers interpreted any questions they might have had. It was quite satisfying to think we had contributed to their education and promoted good feelings for a change.

When I had been stationed at Fort Knox, Kentucky, in the States, I met a man I knew as Sergeant First Class Jones who was a gunnery instructor. He gave classroom instruction on how to use a tank gunsight and how to zero it in if the sight was off. Back then I considered Sergeant Jones to be a pretty sharp dude, so I wasn't too put out when he was put in charge of our tank for a couple of days. Sergeant Jones was black, but that never bothered me at all. We were a team in Nam no matter what the color of our skin was. After one patrol with Sergeant Jones I had changed my mind about his professionalism. We had a mechanic riding on our tank by the name of Jim Bell, and Jim was a black man also. Jim was on his second tour of duty in Vietnam. His first tour of duty was with the infantry, where he had been shot in the arm by an AK-47. I was riding shotgun as we started for the boonies and Sergeant Jones was the tank commander. Everything seemed to be going normally enough until we got into some thick brush in the middle of VC territory. I looked around and didn't see Jones anywhere. I looked inside of the turret and there was Jones, reading a training manual on how to disassemble and reassemble a .50 caliber machine gun. I was incredulous. Jones had two stripes on me, but I wasn't going to let that slow me down. I said, "What in the hell so you think you're doing down there?" He explained that he was studying a T.M. manual. I said, "I can see that, you dumb bastard. Get your ass back up here." He said I was going to be in bad trouble if I talked to him like that again. I said, "Bullshit! You're the tank commander and here we are going into Charlie country, and you don't even know what the hell is going on. What the hell are you going to do if we get attacked? If we did get hit you wouldn't even know it until it was too damn late!" He was mad as hell at me but he finally came topside. A tank commander has to be able to see what is going on around him in order to react and make the right decisions. I didn't know if this guy was scared or just plain stupid, but I guessed that it was a combination of both. Abe looked at me like I was crazy for chewing out an E-7 like that. He hadn't been here long enough to know that survival takes precedence over rank when you're in the field. Jim Bell just gave me a knowing look. He had been around and he knew what the score was. Later on Jim told me that he approved of my actions and he said, "Toby, we got to get off this tank before that stupid son of a bitch gets us killed." I realized then that Jim was as scared as I was. It's bad enough being in the boonies without having a dumb, green sergeant first class who doesn't know his ass from a hole in the ground in charge.

Later that night, when I noticed that Jones was curled up asleep in the bottom of the tank, I knew that the man was just plain scared to death. No one slept in those hot vehicles over here. We slept on folding cots behind the tank or on the ground. We always had one man standing guard in the T.C. hatch and he damned well better not go to sleep. I understood what Jones was feeling. Hell, we all felt that way, but you had to be able to function and be alert. If you tried to hide from reality you were as good as dead. I couldn't feel sorry for Sergeant Jones because he was risking our lives as well as his own. The next day I had a talk with Lieutenant Solars. I told him about Jones's actions and how I chewed him out. The lieutenant understood perfectly. I said, "I want off that fucking tank or I want Jones off, 'cause I ain't going to let that idiot get me killed!" Lieutenant Solars told me he would see what could be done. Jim and I were never so happy as we were when we pulled back into Cu Chi at the end of that patrol. It was fortunate that we hadn't gotten hit during Jones's first patrol. I don't think he could have handled the situation.

I was never asked to go out on his tank again. If it happened, I would have seriously considered killing him.

Chapter 21

I GOT SET TO GO BACK TO THE FIELD along with the rest of the platoon. We were going out on a regular sweep through Charlie country. Fortunately, Sergeant Jones had been assigned to another tank in our platoon. I would have been happier if he hadn't been put in the same platoon at all, but I could live with the situation as it was. I was over my post-Purple Heart jitters by now and I felt fine. Abe Cabrican and I replenished our ammo supply and stocked our larder with C rations. We had everything shipshape when we pulled out of the perimeter at Cu Chi. We drove for several hours through the dust, brush and heat, not seeing a damn thing but the usual papa sans toiling away in their rice paddies. We had received word that a large body of Vietcong were operating in the area, but for all our searching we had turned up nothing but dust.

As soon as the sun started sliding beyond the horizon, we made for our designated night perimeter. I say designated because headquarters had determined that the VC were headed in our direction and they wanted us in their path as a blocking force. We saw to the placement of our vehicles and began to set up our defense. Abe and I set up our RPG screen and concertina wire first thing. I saw to the placement of our tripflares.

My cousin, Randy Kanitz, had served with the 101st Airborne in 1968, a year before I went to Vietnam, and he gave me a tip on setting our tripflares. I decided to take his advice and try it out that night. He told me that everybody always set out their tripflares parallel to their positions, and the VC had gotten to the point where they expected it. He told me to set out my tripflares running perpendicular to my position if I wanted to get better results. I set out two tripflares; one was running parallel and the other was running perpendicular to my position. I tied them both together so that if either one of them were tripped it would set off both tripflares at once.

Our officers expected us to get hit that night so they had us use our infrared searchlights for the first three or four hours of darkness. We saw no signs of movement, so we finally secured the searchlights for the rest of the night. I had the second watch on guard duty that night. It was a moonless night and my eyes must have been as big as dinner plates as I peered into the darkness. Toward the end of my watch my tripflares went off, lighting up the area to my immediate front. I couldn't see anything, but Charlie is a master at camouflage. I opened up with my fifty caliber and sprayed down the whole area in front of my tank with bullets. I didn't draw any return fire, so the lieutenant ordered me to cease firing. I had awakened the entire perimeter, but it seemed as though it was a false alarm. The lieutenant figured an animal must have set off my tripflares and he was grumbling about me being trigger-happy.

I wasn't so sure about his theory and I stayed alert. Just as everyone got settled in again, I heard that dreaded, hollow, thumping sound of a mortar leaving its tube. I yelled "Incoming!" as I scrambled back into our tank. The mortars started hitting inside our perimeter and all hell broke loose. The VC were making an all-out attack on our position. We all opened up, firing into the darkness or at whatever muzzle flashes we could see. The VC were throwing B-40 rockets, mortars, recoilless rifle, machine gun fire and small arms fire at us from all directions. I was on the back of the tank now with an M-16 rifle and Domingo was in the T.C. hatch firing the fifty. I had a fifty-caliber ammo can full of M-16 magazines so I kept my rifle on full automatic as I fired short bursts into the darkness. I was surprised at my calmness as I methodically searched the area to my front with rifle fire. All at once I saw a large, white ball of fire coming at me from the pitch-black night. It was a B-40 rocket, but it was upon us so fast that I didn't even have time to duck. It missed our tank by scant inches and I could feel the heat sear my face as it swooshed by. I kept right on shooting, hoping I could nail the little bastard with the rocket launcher. I saw another explosion to my left as a recoilless rifle round exploded right in front of the bunker of one of the infantrymen working with us. He was still firing his fifty so I knew he was okay. The attack to our front must have been a diversion, because all of a sudden the VC on the other side of our perimeter really started to pour it on the other tanks on that side. Our number three tank started having trouble with his main gun's recoil system. Every time he fired, his cannon would jump out of battery. The lieutenant ordered our tank to go over and help strengthen the other side of the perimeter since the fire from our side had slowed down. As Domingo started to back out and turn around, I was left in an exposed position on the back of the tank, so I started climbing around to the other side of the turret. Just as I got halfway around, the tank made a lurch and I fell off onto the ground. I still had my rifle in my hand so I decided to stay in our old position to cover the empty slot. I didn't have any cover and I only had one magazine of ammo, so I was more than a little worried about my position. Just then Spooky showed up.

"Spooky" was an AC-47 fixed-wing cargo aircraft with three miniguns mounted on one side of the fuselage.

He started circling our perimeter, firing those miniguns at 6000 rounds per minute for each gun. A minigun looks similar to a six barreled Gatling gun. The barrels are rotated by an electric motor. If the pilot chose to, he could put down 18,000 rounds per minute by firing all three guns at once. To give you an idea of the rate of fire, you would need ten of the old style .30 caliber machine guns firing all at once to equal the volume of fire put out by one minigun. Those miniguns fired so quickly they sounded like an angry dog growling deep in his throat. Every fifth round was a tracer, but it looks like a hose of fire spitting earthward. Those tracers started bouncing around like marbles being dropped on a concrete floor. They seemed so close I decided to back out of there and look for some cover. As I moved back toward the center of the perimeter a medivac started to come in, so I slung my rifle over my shoulder and helped the medics load up the wounded. There were only three, but one man had been hit in the head. I didn't think he would make it, but the human body is capable of absorbing a lot of punishment and still bouncing back. After Spooky left, the night became quiet again. We had beaten them back with only three casualties for ourselves. If that Spooky gunship pilot had landed I'm sure we all would have run out and kissed him.

As the gray dawn slowly lighted up the sky, we began surveying the destruction. One of our personnel carriers had been holed by an RPG, but it was still serviceable enough to drive home. The bunker next to where our tank had been had a fifteen-foot trench running straight at the opening where the recoilless rifle round had plowed its way within a foot of the opening before it exploded. That gunner was sure lucky; two inches higher and he would have had that round in his lap. Sergeant Domingo told me that when the rocket blasted by my side of the tank, he thought that it had got me until he saw that I was still firing away. I admitted that it was a close call, but at the time I didn't even have time to think about it; I was too busy. As it got lighter we counted eight bodies outside our perimeter. A couple of them were only ten feet away from our position. We found numerous blood trails where the dead and wounded had been dragged away under the cover of darkness. We were really disappointed that there were no more bodies than that.

A couple of days later, we were told that reconnaissance teams had found over fifty bodies that we had accounted for, but I don't know if there was any truth to that or not. I wouldn't have been surprised, though. With five tanks and five personnel carriers supported by over thirty infantrymen, plus a Spooky gunship, we laid down one hell of a lot of fire that night. We were well pleased with ourselves as we began to pack everything up. Charlie didn't normally hit an armored outfit that was dug in for the night, other than giving it some harassing fire and running away into the night. He had to have a pretty strong force before he would consider taking us on in a sustained attack. We may have foiled his plans for hitting one of the small fire support bases in the area. None of us had gotten any sleep that night, so we were more than ready to go back to our base camp once we had received orders to do so. I silently thanked my cousin Randy for his advice on tripflares because I truly believe that if it had not been for my tripflares going off when they did, alerting our perimeter, things would have gone much worse for us. Everybody had been awakened and the Vietcong had lost the element of surprise. Randy may well have saved my life that night.

Chapter 22

THE MEN IN MY PLATOON AND I had been standing down for two days to give us a chance to get our equipment and vehicles back in shape. We changed engine oil, replaced worn parts on our tanks and cleaned weapons in preparation for more operations in the bush. On the morning of May 2, 1969, our platoon was called upon to escort and provide security for a platoon of infantry with a Vietcong prisoner. The prisoner supposedly had information about a VC tunnel complex that was being dug in order to infiltrate our base camp at Cu Chi. This was just a milk run for us as it was right outside of our own perimeter and we were not in the least bit worried. We had every kind of support that we would ever need at our fingertips; all we had to do was call in for it. We were all in a jovial mood as we met the unit that we were to escort outside the wire. They had a VC prisoner with them and a South Vietnamese army captain to interpret. Naturally we were all very curious about the POW. They were so damned elusive in the field that most of us had never seen a real live Vietcong soldier. He was pretty scraggly-looking and not very impressive at all. He was barefoot and the only articles of clothing he had on were a green pair of shorts and a black peasant's shirt. He was a very short, skinny man, in his early twenties, and he was so subservient as to seem entirely harmless.

The interpreter was also a young man, but he was much more impressive as far as his physical attributes were concerned. He was an altogether good-looking, well-built man, with a certain neat, military bearing about him. He was a very friendly, courteous man whom I immediately liked.

A Sergeant Stafford was in charge of our tank that day, as Domingo was absent again, gone God knows where. I think he had a sixth sense about when to avoid impending danger. Sergeant Stafford was new to our unit, but he seemed to be a competent, decent man. I liked his attitude and personality right away.

The POW and interpreter boarded our tank along with an American MP. I was riding on the bustle rack with an M-16 in one hand, and a cold beer in the other hand, waiting to see what they would find. We traveled only five hundred yards to the east of the main gate at the northern side of our perimeter as we followed the directions of our POW. He indicated to our interpreter where to stop as he pointed in the general direction of the tunnel. Our tanks made a rough semicircle to provide security and the infantry began to deploy as our POW and his guard dismounted from our vehicle. The South Vietnamese captain stood on the back deck of our tank and I was standing beside him with my rifle at port arms as we watched the prisoner and three infantrymen approach the tunnel site. We were watching intently as the men on the ground walked closer and closer to the tunnel. All at once I saw a bright flash and I felt a blast of heat that seemed as though it had been spawned from the depths of hell. A giant fist struck my body and I was lifted into the air as easily as if I were a piece of paper being blown along by the wind. The next thing I knew I was on the ground. My whole body felt numb and I was gasping for air. I struggled to get my breath back for a few seconds. I then realized that I had been hit. I was sure my legs had been hit, but I couldn't tell how bad it was yet. I fought hard to raise up on my hands to see what had happened to me. As I sat up I stared at my legs in horror. Both of my feet were lying at twisted, unnatural angles. That in itself was enough to make me feel sick, but between my knees and ankles there was nothing left but splinters of white bone and a gory mess that resembled something akin to hamburger. It looked as though the only thing that was holding my feet on was a few ragged, bloodly remnants of my jungle fatigues which I had tucked into my boot tops. I still felt pretty numb, but the pain was starting to filter through the haze of my confused and tortured mind. I then realized that the tanks were firing their machine guns and some of the fire was going over my head. I looked all around, trying to locate my rifle, but it was nowhere to be found. I realized that if any Vietcong came out of that tunnel I would be finished off without a second thought, so I rolled over on my stomach and dragged myself to a more secure area behind the tank. The pain was getting worse and I decided that I had better call for a medic. For some idiotic reason I felt somewhat ridiculous, hollering like a damn fool for the medics, but I gave a couple of tentative, halfhearted shouts. As the pain worsened my shouts got louder and more frantic. Finally a medic cautiously picked his way toward me and he was soon by my side. He set up an IV of blood supplement and proceeded to place tourniquets on both my thighs. I was going into shock, and as I lay behind the tank the exhaust was blowing toward my face. I felt as though I couldn't breathe and I was getting a little panicky. I asked the medics several times to please move me so I could get some fresh air. My shortness of breath was due more to the shock than it was to the tank exhaust, but they finally did move me and I calmed down somewhat. As the medics placed me on a stretcher I told them, "Be careful, don't drop my feet!" I was afraid they would fall off as they lifted me. I guess that I knew then that they were gone, but crazy thoughts kept running through my mind, like, *Doctors are doing some pretty miraculous things nowadays and maybe, just maybe, they can put me back together again.*

I was told that the medivac was on its way, so I watched the sky above me with intent anxiety. I bummed a cigarette off one of the medics, which I smoked as I waited. I nearly sighed with relief as the medivac chopper hovered into view, but then he began to circle. I shouted, "Come on down here, you chickenshit son of a bitch, I'm hurting!" But he circled three times before he made his approach. Every time he circled I became more and more profane. I didn't realize there was still firing going on and he was just checking to make sure that he could get in and out without being shot down. Finally he landed and I was loaded up. The stretchers on the dustoff were stacked in tiers about three or four deep. The man who was on the stretcher below me was really thrashing around. He kicked me in the back two or three times. When I said, "Goddammit, take it easy down there, I'm hurt too!" he settled down and in seconds we were at the Twelfth Evac Hospital at Cu Chi. The medics at the hospital rushed out just as we touched down. They grabbed my stretcher and started running for the emergency room door. I told them to slow down because they were bouncing me around like a sack of potatoes. They slowed to a fast walk and carried me the rest of the way to the emergency room.

Once inside the hospital, I became aware of Abe Cabrican's being there, too. He had been hit himself. It appeared that his right arm had been laid open. The pain had begun to get agonizing for me by now and I was starting to get hysterical. I kept asking the doctors to give me something to put me out. The tears sprang to my eyes of their own accord as I yelled to the doctors, "Give me a shot, a goddamned .45 or anything, but put me out of my misery!" A nurse started asking me for my name, rank, service number, and so on. I told her, "Sergeant Toby L. Brant, RA16998368," and finally I said, "Goddamn, lady, can't we do this later?" It did have the effect of calming me down a little. It was a good thing, because with all my yelling and raising hell, poor Abe was getting hysterical himself. It was probably only twenty minutes from the time I got hit till the doctors finally put me under, but it had seemed like an eternity. Even as I look back upon it today it seems as though it was hours before the doctors put me to sleep, but I know that it was only a few minutes.

It may seem odd, but I never once gave a thought to dying. I never even considered that I might not wake up once I had been put to sleep. I asked the doctors not to send my folks a telegram, that I would write to them the next day. I knew that a telegram would scare them to death. They told me they would comply with my wishes. They wanted me to stay as calm as possible. Of course they sent the telegram anyhow, but I wasn't aware of it. The reason the doctors wouldn't give me anything for the pain at first was because they wanted to stabilize my vital signs before they put me under to operate. I was much closer to death than I had realized.

The first thing the nurse told me when I awoke the next day was, "Sergeant Brant, I'm very sorry to tell you this, but you have lost your legs." I said, "Yeah, I know it." I had known it all along, but I hadn't wanted to face it. Once it had been put to me bluntly I knew there was no avoiding the truth. I was pretty calm as I took the bad news. The one big worry that kept running through my mind was, *How am I ever going to be able to break this kind of news to my Mom and Dad?* These thoughts were still racing through my brain as I succumbed to exhaustion and fell back to sleep.

Chapter23

THE DAY AFTER I WAS WOUNDED I was asked by the nurse who was assigned to me if I wanted her to write a letter home to my folks. I thought about it for a moment and I told her, "No, thanks anyway, but I had better write it myself. My folks would think that I'm too bad off to even write a letter and that would really scare them." So I started to write. I really didn't know how to tell them about what had happened to me. I was still unaware of the fact that a telegram had already been sent. I started off the letter by asking them how they were and all that bullshit. I then told them that I was back in the hospital again and that I had got hit by a booby trap. I stated that I had received a lot of shrapnel in my lower legs and that I hoped it was warm enough to water ski when I got home. I just couldn't bring myself to tell them how bad I had really gotten hit. I was trying to break the news as gently as I could.

That morning I was in a great deal of pain and I kept drifting in and out of a drug-induced sleep. As the day went on I started feeling more and more pain in the area of my abdomen. I started complaining to the head nurse, a gruff but good-hearted lady who appeared to be in her early to mid-forties. I told her, "Something isn't right down there. My stomach is killing me." She informed the doctor in charge of my case, and after a thorough examination he made the decision to perform exploratory surgery on my abdomen. I had been given a heavy sedative just before being brought into the operating room and I was really on cloud nine. I don't know what they gave me but I sure felt good. As the orderly wheeled me into the operating room I was grinning like a Cheshire cat. I yelled, "Hey! Is anyone here from Illinois?" That old army nurse was beginning to think that there was nothing wrong with me. She said, "Damn you, Toby, if you're putting us on about that pain I'm going to kick your butt." The doctors put me to sleep and went to work. They found out that a small piece of steel had entered my abdomen just above the belt line where it had traveled upward at a slight angle and had perforated my small intestine in two places. The damage was not extensive and they had me repaired and stitched up in no time at all. I awoke later that night with a twelve-inch incision down the middle of my stomach and feeling like hell. I was really sore now. My lungs were terribly congested, so the nurses had to force me to cough up any phlegm that had accumulated. I felt as though my insides were being torn apart every time I coughed, but it was just something that had to be endured.

Two days after my surgery they had me sitting up in a wheelchair, and on the third day I was moved out of intensive care and into a regular ward. It wasn't until then that I discovered I had a small wound above my left eye, and one behind my left ear, and still more small places on my stomach and back. The small pieces of steel that had hit me in the back must have bounced off the turret. Some of the men from my platoon came by the hospital for a visit. They told me that I had been hit by a 155mm artillery shell that had been booby trapped. It seems that the infantrymen had stepped on a tripwire as they had walked forward with the VC prisoner. The resulting explosion killed two of the men on the ground and the Vietnamese captain who was standing right beside me on the back deck of the tank. He had been hit in the head and chest and had died instantly. There had been ten or twelve men wounded including myself. I was told that I was the most severely wounded man that had survived. I heard that the VC prisoner was still alive, but that the cheeks of his ass had literally been blown off. He also received severe wounds to his legs and back. This news tickled me to death. I had hoped that the dirty bastard was dead, but at least he hadn't gotten away scot-free.

We had another Vietcong prisoner in our ward who was kept under close guard at all times. I tried several times (unsuccessfully) to talk the MP guarding him into letting me spell him for five minutes or so, but I'm afraid he saw the sinister look in my eyes. He said, "Buddy, there is nothing I would like better, but it would be my ass if this crummy gook should suddenly turn up strangled. I'm sorry, but as much as I would like to turn him over to you guys, I just can't." I knew I hadn't been very realistic, but I did thank the MP for being so understanding.

The hospital staff at the Twelfth Evac was really great, as usual, and I got to see some of the nurses that I had met the first time I had been hospitalized. It was pretty hard on them seeing me back in the hospital again. I am sure they felt like they were beating their heads against the wall when they worked so hard to heal the soldiers being brought in, only to see them go back into combat and get hit again. It was bad enough without having repeat customers. I wasn't too crazy about the idea myself.

One of the Red Cross girls told me I could make a telephone call home if I wanted to. It took nearly twelve hours to get the call through to the States because it had to be relayed by ham radio. I'll bet President Nixon didn't have to wait that long. When the call finally went through

I was glad I had made the effort. I found out that my parents had received a very blunt telegram and Mom was so worried that she was nearly a basket case. I could just barely hear them, but at least they could hear me. They were naturally sick at heart by the loss of my legs, but the telegram had stated that I had received abdominal wounds as well. It didn't go into any details about how bad the abdominal wounds were, so Mom and Dad didn't know whether my guts had been blown out or if I had only needed a Band-Aid. I assured them that my stomach wound was not that serious and that I was getting along fine. That one phone call was worth a million dollars to my folks. It did miracles as far as alleviating their worst fears and settling their nerves. Just to hear my voice was a great reassurance to them at that time.

After I had been in the Twelfth Evacuation Hospital for about six days I was able to gingerly get around the grounds in a wheelchair by myself. There was a small quadrangle in the middle of the hospital buildings where the staff would show outdoor movies at night. I decided to go watch the show. I don't even remember what it was about because I ran across a medic who had once been assigned to my tank platoon. He and another guy had a case of beer beside their chairs and I was warmly invited to join them. I didn't need to be asked twice. I pulled my wheelchair up and started drinking. I consumed about four beers and got so drunk I could hardly sit straight. I felt pretty foolish getting wiped out so easily. I hadn't realized how weakened my body had become from all the punishment it had absorbed. I just barely made it back to my ward under my own power. My doctor had allowed me to have a couple of beers a day for the past two or three days, but this time I had overdone it.

Most of my hours at the hospital were spent in quiet

contemplation of my future. I finally decided that nothing could be done about the loss of my legs so it would do neither myself or anyone else any good for me to lie around and feel sorry for myself. There was only one thing for me to do and that was to get on with my life the best I could. I could still think, make love, and drink beer, so all was not lost. I have always been told that if a person looks around them they can always find other people a whole lot worse off than themselves. The day that I was due to be evacuated to Japan I had that lesson driven home to me. As I waited for a plane at the Twelfth Evac, a man was wheeled in beside me. He had lost both legs above the knees and one arm above the elbow. He told me that all he wanted to do was die. I tried to talk to him and maybe cheer him a little, but nothing I could say would dissuade him. He would only say, "Look at me, just look at me. I'm a freak!" I finally said to him, "Look, buddy, I'm in pretty bad shape myself, but I'll be damned if I'm going to give up." He allowed as how I was in a lot better shape than he was. He was right and I didn't know what else I could say to him. I could only hope that eventually he would be able to reach down inside of himself and find the courage it took to go on living. Many times when I've been depressed and felt like giving up I have thought about that soldier and I counted all of the reasons I knew of why life is worth living. It's not always easy, but life is too precious a gift to throw away.

Chapter 24

SEVERAL OTHER PATIENTS AND I were carried aboard a cargo plane and transported to the Bien Hoa Air Force Base. We had to wait overnight and all the next day at the hospital there until transportation became available to take us to Japan. I was slated to go to the 106th General Hospital in Yokohama. When our plane was ready we were taken out on our stretchers and loaded aboard, stretchers and all, on large racks. These racks were built along both sides of the fuselage, and a double row was situated down the center. We were stacked four and five tiers high. Our plane was a large four-engined cargo craft called a C-141 Galaxy. Once everyone had been strapped down we taxied out and said farewell to Vietnam forever. During our flight we had nurses and doctors hovering over us constantly, keeping a close check on everyone all the way to Japan. Little did I know that when I left Vietnam I was leaving the last decent hospital I would see for quite a spell. The conscientiousness of the doctors and nurses at Cu Chi was beyond compare.

We landed in Japan and from the airport we were taken by chopper to the 106th General Hospital. My whole body was stiff from riding that stretcher for so long, so it felt pretty good to be back in a real bed. My bandages hadn't been changed in four days and I was really dreading having them unwrapped. I knew that they would be stuck to my wounds pretty bad. The wounds on the stumps of my legs had been left open so that the dirt and infection would be allowed to drain. There had been a lot of dirt and debris forced into my wounds from the force of the explosion. I had asked the doctor in charge if he would put me to sleep before he changed my dressings. To my great relief he decided to comply with my wishes.

We had one nurse on our ward who had severe emotional problems. She had a real big chip on her shoulder because she was unmarried and pregnant. She was grouchy, nervous, and overly defensive about her predicament. The woman was paranoid to the point of accusing everyone of making fun of her and talking about her all the time. This of course simply was not true. Her being knocked-up was the least of our worries. That gal would forget to give us any medication for pain sometimes, and she constantly screwed up. She had no damned business trying to take care of a bunch of guys whose nerves were already shot all to hell. One afternoon I tried to joke with her a little and lighten her mood. I called her Florence Nightingale. She really hit the ceiling. I was accused of calling her a whore and I don't know what all else. I don't know where she got her information, but she told me that Florence Nightingale was not only a famous nurse but that she had been a prostitute as well. I said, "Well, Jesus Christ! Do you expect me to know all that crap?" I couldn't help it because she had a guilty conscience, and from that time forward I did my best to avoid even speaking to her.

We had a warped son of a bitch at the 106th who was a medic. He took a perverse pleasure in filling a syringe with water and squirting helpless patients with it. I tried to smack him in the mouth one day but I was too sore to move fast enough and I missed him. He then threatened me with bodily harm. I had been a given a miniature bayonet letter opener with the Twenty-Fifth Infantry Division crest on it as a souvenir before I had left Vietnam.

I took this bayonet from my personal items and hid it beneath my pillow. The next time he came around with his syringe I pulled out that bayonet and told him if he squirted me again I was going to gut him. He took me at my word and never squirted me again.

The third day I was at the 106th we went through a mild earthquake. Being from the midwestern part of the United States, I was not used to having a building shake beneath me. I wasn't able to run and it left me feeling pretty nervous. I was being shipped back to the United States in one more day and I was never so happy to leave a place in my life. I had had it with Japan and I was ready to leave my distraught nurse, sadistic medic, and shaking buildings behind.

I have an uncle who was a chief petty officer in the United States Navy. His ship was in Japan at the same time I was hospitalized there and his wife, my dad's younger sister, had somehow gotten the word to him about me getting hurt. He tried his best to find me, but he had one major problem: he couldn't remember my first name. My Aunt Sharon had always called me by a nickname; therefore, Uncle Everett had to call his wife in Hawaii to find out my real first name. He finally found out where I was staying, but by the time he got there I had already been shipped back to the good ole USA. My uncle had missed seeing me by only an hour or two.

I went to the United States in the same manner that I had been transported to Japan, in a large cargo plane, lying on a stretcher. Those stretchers can get awfully uncomfortable during a long trip, and I was totally exhausted by the time our plane reached the States. After the plane had landed we were loaded onto a bus which had racks to hold our stretchers. Our bus driver must have hit every bump, chuck hole and rut in the road on the way to Walter

Reed Army Hospital. The bus felt as though it had no springs at all, it rode that rough. I was bouncing all over that stretcher like a rubber ball. I yelled at the driver, "Slow this damn thing down!" I might as well have talked to the wind for all the good it did me. After a brutal, bone-jarring trip to the hospital we were unloaded; then we had to wait to be assigned to a permanent ward. Each patient was allowed to make a three-minute phone call to let his family know he had made it back to the United States. My family had been waiting a long time under a great deal of stress to hear that news. A great many people from my hometown chipped in with whatever money they could afford and donated it to my mother and father so that they were able to afford the cost of the trip to Washington, D.C. It really made me feel great to know that so many people cared enough to help. You really find out who your true friends are when the chips are down. I am forever grateful to those kind of people from Charleston and the surrounding area.

There were so many wounded soldiers coming home from Vietnam in 1969 that it staggered the mind. I was taken to a large, open ward that held about sixty patients. Every man in that ward was an amputee. They had one arm, one leg, both arms or both legs missing, and in some cases there were men who had been blinded, and men who had all of their limbs missing. There were many men who survived Vietnam that would never have had a chance in earlier wars, due to the efficiency of the medivac helicopters. It could be a pretty sobering sight for the uninitiated. People have been known to pass out from the initial shock of seeing so many young men maimed for life.

The doctor in charge of our ward was a woman. Major McKay was a serious, no-nonsense lady. She also had the compassion of a slaughterhouse meat cutter. She was rough almost to the point of being sadistic. When Dr. McKay changed bandages she didn't unwrap them gently—she ripped them off. It didn't matter to her whether she caused her patients any pain or not, so long as she got the job done. I actually saw her nip off the bone that was protruding from the end of one man's stump while he was still awake and in his bed. She didn't take him to an operating room, nor did she use any kind of anesthesia other than aspirin as she performed this operation. He had to bite down on his pillow to keep from screaming out in pain. I was having a lot of trouble with phantom pains, as was everyone else in the ward, but when I asked her if anything could be done to alleviate the pain, she said, "You'll just have to toughen them up," meaning my stumps. With that statement she tightened up her fist and rapped sharply two times on the end of my raw stump. I still hadn't had my wounds closed up as of yet and I nearly jumped straight into the air. I said, "If you ever do that again I'm going to punch you right in the mouth." She just laughed and went on her way. I couldn't believe that bitch. I was beginning to think I had been sent to Dachau instead of Walter Reed.

The medics at Walter Reed weren't much better, but most of them did try to be a little more gentle. They could be very lax about washing their hands between working on patients, though. I was afraid they would spread infection from patient to patient, so I said, "To hell with it," and I started changing my own dressings. This worked out pretty well because it relieved them of the duty of working on one more patient and I was a lot more gentle with myself. Whenever Dr. McKay made her rounds and started to yank at my bandages I would just say, "Hold on, I'll do it myself."

My parents came to see me as quick as they could and they stayed for over a week. It was wonderful to see them again and I know they felt a lot better after they got to see me. They realized that I was in good spirits and that I was in no danger of dying. Dad even smuggled in a few beers from time to time. This whole experience had been pure hell for them and I did everything I could to relieve them of their fears. Mom and Dad were both in a lot better frame of mind by the time they headed back home.

Dad had heard about some of the lousy treatment we had received at the hospital, so when he got home he fired a letter off to Congressman William Springer, raising cain about the situation. Congressman Springer started an investigation right away. Within a month I was called into a large office where I was confronted by a general and three other high-ranking oficers. I was told about the investigation and they said they were looking into the situation. They told me I needed to sign this form to verify that I had talked to them. I was nervous and intimidated as hell from being around all that brass and I signed the paper without a second thought. I found out much later that I had signed a release form stating that an investigation had been held and that everything was okay. In other words, I had screwed up royally and lost the only chance I had of forcing the situation into the open.

I spent nearly three months at Walter Reed. Toward the end of my stay I was allowed to go on a twenty-four-hour pass along with a couple of my buddies. One of them, Larry Robbins, had lost an arm, was blinded in one eye, and had lost three fingers from his remaining hand. He had been hit by an RPG. Ralph Taylor, the other guy, had taken a few slugs in his back from a VC machine gun and was confined to a wheelchair for the time being. I was minus both legs and confined to a wheelchair myself, so we made a fine-looking crew as we went on down the street. It sort of reminded me of that old saying about "the blind leading the blind." The first place we stopped at was a bar, naturally. We got several stares as we struggled in past the door, but I'm happy to say the patrons of that place were a great bunch of guys. We didn't have to pay for a single drink the whole time we were there. This made us feel very good and we were really grateful to those kind gentlemen. Later on we bought a bottle of booze to go and rented ourselves a hotel room in one of the swankier establishments in that area. It sure felt good to be out on our own for a change and to lie down in a nice, soft bed without rubber sheets. We got ourselves a delicious gourmet meal and had a great time enjoying the sights and sounds of freedom for the first time in many months. By the time we got back to Walter Reed we all had some real dandy hangovers, but our liberty had been worth every bit of it.

I had been asking for a transfer to the Indianapolis Veterans Hospital because it was located much closer to my hometown. Once Congressman Springer started his investigation the higher-ups were probably only too glad to get rid of me. I always was something of a nonconformist, and the army doesn't like to have people make waves. Nothing could have made me happier than to get away from that place. Maybe the presidents, generals, and congressmen got first-class treatment at Walter Reed, but I can sure testify that if you happened to be a lowly enlisted man the treatment was considerably poorer.

I began my journey to Indianapolis aboard a rickety, old DC-3, the passenger version of the same AC-47 cargo plane used as a Spooky gunship in Vietnam. Every time we hit an air pocket I felt like I was going to lose my stomach. I had a long, roundabout trip with several stops, including an overnight stay at Scott A.F.B. in Illinois before I made it to the Indianapolis Veterans Administration Hospital. After all the time I had been at Walter Reed I still had infection in both of my stumps. When I arrived at the hospital the staff there got right to work. The doctors and nurses at the V.A. hospital were much, much better than I had had at Walter Reed. They were on par with the doctors and nurses I had left in Vietnam, which means that they were pretty darn good. Within three or four weeks the infection in my stumps were totally cleared up and I was ready to start a series of operations to close the ugly, nasty wounds on the remnants of my legs.

I was now able to go home on weekends most of the time, and many of my friends were able to come and visit me. This made life in the hospital much more bearable for me. I had not been at Indianapolis too long when I received the surprise of my life. My old platoon leader, Lieutenant Rich Solars, and Lieutenant Green, my old executive officer from Vietnam, came to visit with me. They had both been promoted to captain and they were stationed at Fort Benjamin Harrison, right outside town. It was really good to see them. I was thrilled to death that they had taken the time to visit with me and show their concern.

Once the doctors were able to start operating on my stumps it didn't take very long for me to heal up. In two month's time, and after four operations, I was getting in pretty good shape. I had been measured for my new legs and it was only a matter of time until I could be released. I had been confined to a bed and wheelchair for so long that I was really anxious to get mobile again. Once I got my artificial legs, I worked very hard to master the techniques that would enable me to get around. It took me many hours of pain and agonizing labor, but I was determined to succeed and nothing was going to stop me from reaching my goals. On the morning of November 5, 1969, I was released from the hospital at Indianapolis. I had been in four different hospitals for six long months and I felt like a convicted man getting a reprieve from prison. I didn't think I would ever see the day, but here it was, and I had a lot of living to do and a lot of lost time to make up for. The first thing I did was to go out and buy one of the hottest, fastest, sleekest-looking cars on the market. I wanted some wheels that looked great and would run like a bat out of hell. I wanted plenty of freedom and I never wanted to be tied down and helpless ever again. I didn't realize it at the time, but my troubles were far from over. My personal battle for peace of mind had just begun. I had changed in many ways, and my physical wounds were only half of the story.

Chapter 25

GETTING OUT OF THE HOSPITAL and coming home was a great pleasure for me at first, but it didn't take long for me to become embittered. I soon had it driven home to me that I was only twenty years old. It was illegal for me to go to a bar or to buy a drink. After all I had been through, I couldn't even buy a beer. I had to have a co-signer before any bank or lending institution would give me a loan. I was old enough to put my life on the line for my country, but I wasn't old enough to vote. I was livid with rage. I had been old enough to be sent to Vietnam, old enough to lead men into combat, and old enough to get my ass blown away, yet I didn't even have the right to vote against the very people who had sent me to Vietnam. It seemed to me that there was very little justice in the world.

One of the first things I did when I got home was to buy myself a gun. I had been accustomed to carrying a gun and I felt almost defenseless without one, especially since my legs were gone. I bought a .44 magnum, the largest pistol in the shop. Fortunately, I had the good sense to never use it on anybody and I eventually put it away so I wouldn't be tempted to use it.

I had troubles with nightmares for quite a while. One nightmare that kept recurring was particularly frightening. I would find myself lying in a foxhole and see incoming rounds landing all around me, and then I would see the Vietcong coming at my position. I didn't have any legs, so when I would see a Vietcong soldier throw a grenade at me I couldn't run away, and the grenade was out of reach. I would wake up in a cold sweat while waiting for that damn grenade to go off. I always woke up just in time, and I was always left with such a feeling of helplessness.

Going out with my old friends made me realize just how much I had changed. It seemed as though we had nothing in common anymore. The only things I talked about were Vietnam, the army, guns, VC, and tanks. They didn't have the slightest conception of what I was talking about. They knew nothing about Vietnam, and I had lost track of all the latest fads, songs, and trends. Furthermore, those things no longer had any meaning to me. No one understood when I tried to talk about what it was like in Nam. My old friends seemed like strangers to me, and I must have seemed the same to them. I eventually bottled up most of my feelings and stopped talking about Vietnam.

One of the first things I saw when I got home was an antiwar demonstration right in my hometown. I didn't really expect a parade or anything, but this was too damn much. Eastern Illinois University is located in Charleston, where I live, and an antiwar rally was being staged on the main road that passes by the campus. All these people were out stopping traffic and passing out leaflets. As I stopped at a stop sign, a hippie-looking character stuck his head in my window as he tossed me a leaflet. He said, "They are bombing the poor women and children of North Vietnam and we have to stop these baby killers." I lost my temper as I threw the leaflet back into his face. I said, "Get out of my window, you dirty son of a bitch, or I'll tear your head off!" Needless to say he withdrew his head and said, "Okay, brother," and he left me alone. I was so mad I was shaking. Who in the hell did these draft-dodging punks think they were to call us "baby killers?" I felt that they were within their rights to have a peaceful protest, and even to put down that lousy war, but they damn sure had no right to slander the men who had fought and died in Vietnam, men who were just doing their duty the best way they knew how.

I would get depressed easily back then and I drank heavily night and day. I used booze as an escape because getting drunk brought oblivion. It got to the point where the only people I hung around with were war veterans or men who were out of work and hung around the bars all day long. I didn't like to drink alone. My drinking partners were more often as not unsavory characters who got into trouble a lot and who tended to use me or to take advantage of me at times. I had been awarded a substantial pension from the Veterans Administration, and it was well known that I about always had money to buy drinks.

I had looked all over the place trying to find a job, but every place that I put in an application either turned me down outright, or they would call me in for an interview to make it look good and then turn me down. Once it was known that I had wooden legs I would be told that I couldn't handle the job, or that their insurance wouldn't cover me. They wouldn't even give me an opportunity to try out. I eventually began to lose all hope of ever having a decent job.

In a strange way I almost missed the excitement of combat. There is something about living on the thin edge of disaster that really makes a person feel alive. Every moment that you cheat death is a victory. You feel an intensity that cannot be equaled even though you may be scared to death. It's hard to explain, but maybe it's the same feeling that race car drivers experience. I suppose that is the reason why I would drive my car like a maniac. I missed that intensity. I actually enjoyed the danger of pushing my car to the limit.

The longer I was home, the more bitter I became. I

felt as though I were less than a man sometimes because I had lost my legs. I had a bad habit of picking fights just to prove to myself, and the world, that I was no pushover and that I could still hack it. I was a pretty strong guy and I was also lucky as hell, so I usually won the fights I got into. However, it is a lousy feeling to sober up and then have to go apologize to all of your friends the next day for being such an asshole. I hardly ever felt sorry for myself, but I had a terrible chip on my shoulder, and I would get depressed so easily sometimes that it was scary.

I married my first wife a year after I got home, but my marriage was destined for failure. My wife hadn't really been ready for marriage and neither was I. I had gotten married way too soon. I didn't give myself time to get used to being home. I hadn't adjusted to the idea of being handicapped, and then, on top of everything else, I had to try to get accustomed to being married. It was just too much for me to handle at one time. I would go out drinking with the guys and stay gone for two and three days at a time without coming home or calling. My wife had to put up with my dark moods and frequent bouts with the law because of my fighting and drinking. I loved her, but I just couldn't seem to get my act together. It gradually tore our marriage apart. She wasn't perfect either, but most of the blame falls upon my shoulders. I started to settle down after a while, but by the time that happened it was too late to salvage my marriage. I found out that she had started seeing another man. This hit me like a ton of bricks, and after eight long years she asked me for a divorce and I gave my wife her freedom. The only thing of any value we have to show for our time together is a beautiful daughter whom I love more than life itself.

When South Vietnam finally fell, I was watching the whole painful process on television. I cried tears of frustration and rage as I watched the North Vietnamese Army tanks roll into Saigon and crash through the U.S. embassy gates. It tore me apart. It should have been our tanks rolling into Hanoi that day. I felt as though I had been stabbed in the back by our inept leaders for not letting us win that war, and for not letting us fight it as it should have been fought. I thought of all the men who had died and given up their lives for nothing. I had lost my legs for nothing. We had naught to show for all the years of blood, sweat and tears we had shed for that two-bit country. The only thing left was bitter memories. What a terrible waste of one of our country's most valuable assets, the thousands of young men who would never be able to realize their hopes, dreams, and aspirations. I sincerely hoped that if we had accomplished nothing else, that maybe our country had learned its lesson about getting us into any more wars that the politicians and tinhorn brass were unwilling to win.

I made up my mind that day that I was going to do everything in my power to prevent our involvement in any useless wars in the future that our political leaders might try to get us involved in. When President Ronald Reagan decided to send troops into the war-torn country of Lebanon, I spoke out against it. I circulated petitions, spoke on television, and I wrote the president and the Congress expressing my outrage and displeasure with the situation. Finally, after hundreds of U.S. Marines had been killed needlessly, our country pulled together and withdrew the so-called peace-keeping force. This was probably not due to any of my actions, but at least I had tried. If nothing else, it had helped to salve my conscience. This time I had not sat on my hands and done nothing.

I have since remarried and found a semblance of normalcy. I have learned to live with the memories of Vietnam and accept life for what it is. My present wife and I are very happy together. We have a log home in the country that we share with the birds and other wildlife in the area. I still have fits of depression at times, and once in a while I have a bad dream about Vietnam, but now my dark moods are much less frequent, as are the nightmares. I have slowed my drinking to an acceptable level and I have learned to live with myself and my memories without feeling too much bitterness. It has been difficult dredging up the specter of the past, but maybe if enough people read these pages they will eventually say, "Enough! We want no more Vietnams." Then my efforts will have been worthwhile, and the young men who gave their lives in Vietnam will not have died in vain.

GLOSSARY

AIT: Advanced individual training.

AK-47: Standard enemy weapon. A Soviet- and Chinese-produced semiautomatic or automatic 7.62mm assault rifle.

APC OR PC: Armored personnel carrier, M-113.

ARVN: Army of the Republic of Vietnam. A South Vietnamese soldier or marine. Phoneticized "Arvin."

B-40: A communist-bloc rocket-propelled grenade launcher. Also the rounds-fired B-40 rockets. Capable of penetrating armor.

BOONIES: The field, the brush, the jungle. Any place outside of a base camp, fire support base, city or village.

C-40: A powerful plastic explosive.

CHARLIE: The Vietcong. Also the military phonetic for the letter C.

CHERRY: A new troop.

CHIEU HOI: Vietnamese for "Open Arms," an amnesty program to encourage enemy soldiers to rally to the RVN.

CHINOOK: A large twin-rotor cargo helicopter, CH-47, often referred to as a "Shithook."

CLAYMORE: Antipersonal mines with a one-pound charge of C-4 behind 600 small steel balls.

CO: Commanding officer.

COBRA: An assault helicopter, AG-1H.

C-RATIONS: Combat rations.

DUST-OFF: Medical evacuation by helicopter.

FIRE SUPPORT BASE: A small base camp built to protect an artillery battery.

GOOK: A derogatory term for Vietcong, NVA, or any Oriental.

GUNSHIP: Heavily-armed helicopter, used primarily to support troops.

HOOTCH: A Vietnamese dwelling and any building used to house troops.

KIA: Killed in action.

KIT CARSON SCOUT: A Vietnamese working with an American combat unit, usually a former Vietcong.

LRRP: Long-range reconnaisance patrol("Lurp").

M-16: Standard U.S. Army rifle used in Vietnam. A gas-operated, air-cooled automatic/semiautomatic assault weapon weighing 7.6 pounds with a twenty-round magazine. Maximum range 2350 meters. Maximum effective range 460 meters. Automatic firing rate 650-700 rounds per minute; sustained automatic firing rate 100-200 rounds per minute.

M-48 A3: Standard heavy tank used in Vietnam, weighing fifty-two tons and armed with a 90mm cannon, a fifty caliber machine gun, and a 7.62 machine gun. Propelled by a V-12 diesel engine.

M-60: Standard American light machine gun. A gas-operated, air-cooled, belt-fed automatic machine gun.

M-79: An American single-shot 40mm grenade launcher.

MEDIVAC: Medical evacuation by helicopter.

MIA: Missing in action.

MINIGUN: An electric Gatling gun having six barrels. Capable of firing 6000 rounds per minute.

NAM: Vietnam.

NCO: Noncommissioned officer.

NUMBA ONE: The best, slang.

NUMBA TEN: The very worst, slang.

NVA: North Vietnamese Army, also North Vietnamese soldier.

122: A 122mm communist rocket capable of traveling, with booster, twenty-two kilometers.

RPG: Rocket-propelled grenade.

SLICKS: Lightly-armed Huey helicopters used for transporting troops.

STAND-DOWN: A combat unit's return from the boonies to base camp for refitting and rest.

TET: Vietnamese Lunar New Year holiday.

VC: Vietcong.

WIA: Wounded in action.

WORLD: The USA or any place other than Vietnam.